Helping Children to be Skilful Communicators

From Birth to Three

Ann Roberts and Avril Harpley

 David Fulton Publishers

David Fulton Publishers Ltd
The Chiswick Centre, 414 Chiswick High Road, London W4 5TF

www.fultonpublishers.co.uk
www.onestopeducation.co.uk

First published in Great Britain in 2006 by David Fulton Publishers

10 9 8 7 6 5 4 3 2 1

David Fulton Publishers is a division of Granada Learning Limited, part of ITV plc.

British Library Cataloguing in Publication Data
A catalogue record for this book is available from the British Library.

ISBN: 1 84312 449 1

EAN: 978 184312 449 8

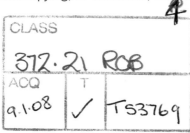

Typeset by FiSH Books, Enfield, Middx.
Printed and bound in Great Britain

Contents

Acknowledgements

We are indebted to the following for their kind permission to use their photographs:

Helen Bilton, Karen James, Jackie Marsh, Anne Wilson, Maggie Woonton and colleagues at Brent council to include Figure 4.5, taken from their book *Learning Outdoors* (David Fulton Publishers, 2005).

Learning through Landscapes and the Glebe Day Nursery in Larkfield, for permission to use Figure 1.6, taken from Gail Ryder Richardson's book *Creating a Space to Grow* (David Fulton Publishers, 2005).

Hugh Shankland, the North Tyneside ICAN specialist nursery for children with speech and language difficulties and the parents who gave permission for photos of their children to be used in the book *Communication Counts; Speech and Language Difficulties in the Early Years* (David Fulton Publishers, 2002). Nursery staff who collaborated with Fleur Griffiths in creating this book.

To the parents of Jasmine and Matthew – many thanks!

Ann and Avril

Introduction

Communicating our thoughts, wants and needs is crucial for our well-being as humans. Becoming a skilful communicator enables us to listen and respond to others, be sociable and develop positive relationships. Supporting babies and toddlers to become skilful communicators is vital, as it gives them the benefit of a good start and prepares them for their future. However, it requires effort, skill and empathy.

This book uses the framework of *Birth to Three Matters* (DfES, 2002) and adds to it some effective everyday suggestions for activities which parents and carers can try with their baby or toddler. Every child is unique and some children develop their language skills at different rates. Adults need to act as interested enablers and through acknowledging and encouraging children they will engender confidence. These are the intentions behind the activities and suggestions for children.

In this book the activities are based around easily accessible everyday items in order to encourage carers to use these objects to support and reflect the home environment within the setting. Simple role-play opportunities, such as using boxes and cloths, encourage open-ended play and exploration, enabling children to communicate what is in their mind. Imagination, creativity and language are all interconnected.

By posing challenges and questions to staff, readers are invited to reflect on their own practice and think about how they can communicate more effectively with babies and toddlers and assist their developing skills.

How can we help children to be skilful communicators?

Talking to babies and toddlers is very important and everyday opportunities such as dressing, changing and mealtimes provide ideal opportunities or scenarios. Reminders of this are to be found in the activity sections of the book and attached to them are some specific ideas on what to do. Singing and talking to babies and toddlers at these times initiates, sustains and invites communication. Nappy changing and potty times can become very clinical if they are just moments for adults to deal with babies' and toddlers' bodily functions. Babies and toddlers pick up on this and these times can become tearful, uncomfortable and unwelcome events.

Signals and signs

Language or communication is not just about speech as many people might assume; it is also about body language. Your body language and the quality of your voice is all that babies have to go on. All babies communicate well before they know any words. As *Birth to Three Matters* suggests, they are 'Finding a Voice' – an important part of the process of becoming a skilful communicator.

Parents, family members and carers all need to play their part. Recognising signals that a baby is giving out helps us to understand her needs and respond to these signals in order to reinforce these initial forms of communication. To be a skilful communicator, then, you need to make eye contact and observe facial gestures as well as watching body movements. A baby can signal her displeasure by turning her head, closing her lips and tightening her body – this signals 'No, I do not want this!' Rouse Selleck (1995) captures this beautifully by saying 'Although most infants do not learn to talk until their second year, their voices are there for us to hear from birth'.

Currently in the UK there are many different cultures and languages and communication with children from diverse or unfamiliar backgrounds can appear to be challenging. It will require a sensitive understanding and appreciation of others in order to meet their individual needs. Children's early development is learning through play. Quality sensory experiences that have a very practical base are ideal as these encourage children's desire to communicate, whatever their language.

Within communication, sharing meaning is important and programmes using signs or signs and words are currently being recognised by professionals as a useful support to communication (not as a replacement). Baby signing is used in some settings in the UK and in the USA. Signing is being used with parents and staff, in early years settings and even in schools, as a part of an overall programme to develop very early communication between babies and adults. Enabling children to become effective communicators by offering them a wide selection of opportunities and options allows them to find their own unique voice.

Conclusions

Many opportunities to communicate often just happen during everyday events and so require little or no resources, just a human response. Seizing on what children find interesting and encouraging this means that adults have to be observant, responsive and accepting. At times, an adult can create a stimulus to excite young children's curiosity or to elicit a response, for example by providing bubbles and balloons.

There needs to be an investment made by adults in order to support children to be effective communicators. This book reinforces this again and again as it provides many activity ideas for the adult to take and use, adapt according to the child and enjoy.

When children learn to speak they say the funniest things and this is the reward and pleasure we get once they start to experiment with words and ideas as their communication skills develop.

Acknowledging their efforts and encouraging them in a positive way builds their confidence and skills and sets them well on the road to becoming a skilful communicator with much to say about their world and in their world.

How to use this book

This book has been written with a practical focus in mind. Practitioners need ideas to use with babies and toddlers. They are busy people and have limited resources at their disposal. The connections made with *Birth to Three Matters* at the beginning of each chapter are designed to support them as they plan and use the documents on a daily basis.

After an introduction, each chapter contains six numbered parts, each one subdivided into sections. The first two sections of each part look at babies and toddlers. The baby section covers from 0 to 18 months and the toddlers' section runs from 18 to 36 months. Both provide practical activities. Obviously, the practitioner will recognise that every child is unique and so adaptations to some of the suggested activities will be necessary. Safety is very important and so cautionary advice is offered throughout the book. If children have specialist needs, readers will need to take these into consideration before using the activities and make an informed safety decision on how to use them in their situation.

Following the activities is a section on the outcomes for the child. The points are designed to help us fully recognise the importance of the child in everything that is offered. If we are intending to help children to communicate, we need to assess how well we are doing this from the child's point of view. Ofsted also focuses on this within its inspection framework and so this will assist practitioners in their evaluations and their preparation for an Ofsted visit.

The focus points that follow are to make us as adults draw some thoughts and feelings together about the practical activities, their purpose, the impact they have and how can all this be built on for the child. They are intended to encourage the reader to consider, question and reflect.

Staff discussion is important. Talking about what we do and trying to make sense of it with others helps us to improve the quality and standard of our work. If we want children to be effective communicators, we need to see how our role is fitting into the overall picture and how effective we are being.

Finally, each chapter concludes with a list of references. These references are linked to three key documents: *National Standards for Under 8s Day Care and Childminding (Full Day Care)* (DfES/DWP, 2003), *Birth to Three Matters* (DfES, 2002), and *Every Child Matters* (DfES, 2003). These are intended to assist the reader in making connections between practice and theory.

References

DfES (Department for Education and Skills) (2002) *Birth to Three Matters: A Framework to Support Children in their Earliest Years.* London: DfES.

DfES (Department for Education and Skills) (2003) *Every Child Matters.* London: DfES.

DfES (Department for Education and Skills)/DWP (Department for Work and Pensions) (2003) *National Standards for Under 8s Day Care and Childminding (Full Day Care).* London: DfES.

Selleck, R. (1995) *Managing Change.* London: National Children's Bureau.

Talk to Your Baby (National Literacy Trust) – www.talktoyourbaby.org.uk

1 Being sociable

Introduction

Humans need to be able to form positive relationships with others and good communication skills are crucial for this to happen. Without good communication skills a child's progress through life and learning is delayed. Babies engage in two-way communications from birth and some are highly competent at giving and responding to signals.

Only a very small percentage of our communication is conveyed through speech, although words have the power to inspire, influence, comfort and hurt. Subtle messages are conveyed physically through our body language, gestures and facial expressions and verbally through the tone and intonation of our voice as well as the vocabulary we use. Today we are surrounded by a wide variety of media and each one is a powerful medium for communication – oral, aural, written and visual. It can be through print, music, painting, dance or any combination of these as well as speech and gesture.

Depending on our own unique life experiences we interpret and process messages in our own way and may distort them to fit in with our thinking, our values, prejudices and generalisations. As practitioners we need to help children to become effective communicators so that they can form positive friendships and express themselves and their feelings clearly and with confidence.

Both *Birth to Three Matters* (DfES, 2002) and the *Curriculum Guidance for the Foundation Stage* (QCA, 2000) highlight the need for practitioners to develop effective communication skills and those of the children in their care. Sure Start Personal, Social and Emotional Development (PSED) materials provide practitioners with useful exercises for learning how to develop the essential building blocks of social skills interaction and developing relationships. *Communicating Matters* (DfES, 2005) is a training package offered to practitioners to develop their skills in supporting language.

Children's early experiences, whether positive or negative, can influence them throughout their lives; they affect their self-esteem, their ability to forge relationships and to learn. Children who develop good social and communication skills have a better chance in life.

1. Social contact

Being physically close and making eye contact, using touch or voice provides an ideal opportunity for early 'conversations' between adults and babies; and one baby and another.

(Birth to Three Matters)

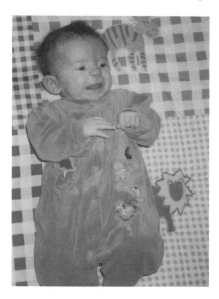

Babies

Babies form close attachments and when left in day care, or with other family members, multiple attachments need to be made. There are many theories around attachment. One of these is the sensitive responsiveness theory (Schaffer and Emerson, 1964). They point out that babies form attachments to those who are aware of their social needs and interact with them rather than those who largely ignore them except when they are crying. Naming a key person for each baby means nothing unless work on attachments is happening every time there is contact. Being close, using eye contact or touch turns these into 'early conversations' and ensures that being together supports healthy attachments.

Practical activities

- Collect some rhymes and songs that ensure physical contact is being made – such as 'Pat-a-cake' or 'Round and round the garden like a teddy bear'. Alternate these and have a short time daily when these are shared.

- Ensure that carers are aware of favourite toys and when babies are anxious offer these alongside a cuddle – the texture, taste or smell of a comforter becomes recognised early on. Discuss with parents/other carers how particular babies are comforted as they are all unique.

- Make up a 'treasure basket' with a variety of soft brushes, such as men's shaving brushes, soft pastry brushes. Stroking the skin is soothing and comforting.
- Allow babies to experience sand play – running their fingers through the sand is a soothing sensory experience.
- Collect lots of different materials and textures and let babies feel and touch them – use appropriate sounds as you share the experience with them.

Toddlers

It is important to allow toddlers time to adjust to a new setting and build up a positive attachment to their key person. Some toddlers have not yet learnt the skills of socialisation and may not be able to express their fears and confusion when left in a setting. They need sensitive support, patience and understanding so that they are able to talk about their concerns. Children who are confident and have positive self-esteem make friends more easily.

Practical activities

- Develop settling-in procedures for parents and new children. For example, arrange for parents to spend time with their toddler in the setting before gradually taking a less active role, leaving the setting for longer periods until their child has made the adjustments.
- Welcome children into the setting with pleasure and interest.
- Establish consistent routines so that children can anticipate what will happen and what they are expected to do.
- Arrange activities so that children can work alongside others, for example sand and water play, sharing jugs and bottles etc. and large equipment that needs another person to play with, e.g. a see-saw, parachute play, trucks that need a 'pusher'.
- Focus on children's strengths and praise those who are playing well together using positive comments about their behaviour.
- Set up turn-taking games and simple rules about shared equipment, for example wheeled toys.
- Allow children to choose who they wish to sit with or play with.
- Support those lone children who have not yet learnt to play with others by joining them, partnering them and promoting collaborative play skills.

Outcomes for the child

- Appropriate touching and physical contact is part of being close.
- Being together is part of conversational behaviour.
- Learning to play and work with other children.
- Developing social interaction.

Focus points

Think about how different cultures approach being physically close in terms of sociable and effective communication and how this will impact on the child. Some key persons may be concerned about physical closeness and how the boundaries are defined. Observing staff in situ with babies provides this evidence and may help staff to develop professionally. Children learn by imitation and copying good role models. It is important that the adults in a setting provide positive behaviour codes.

Staff discussion

- Ask staff to revisit the work on attachment covered by John Bowlby in the 1950s – *Child Care and the Growth of Love* (Bowlby, 1953) (they may have covered this on their initial training) – and discuss the relevance it has today given the changing world we live in.
- If you work in a setting, discuss the key person's approach and the effect on a child's well-being. If you are not in day care, then research some of the work on attachment by Peter Elfer in the late 1990s.
- Observe, track and record how often a child makes contact with other children, how well he co-operates during activities. Note any developing peer relationships, friendships and positive behaviour.

2. Making contact

Babies use their developing physical skills to make social contact.

(*Birth to Three Matters*)

 Babies

As babies start to make contact various motor sensory and cognitive developments are also taking place. Once a baby understands how to move her arms and legs to grasp and reach for objects she begins to appreciate that she can do this with other human beings in order to interact and gain a response. Babies' growing awareness of their muscles and senses alongside the development of patterns in sight, sound and language are all promoted by opportunities for strong social contact.

Practical activities

- Spend some time talking to an individual baby and while talking gently move her arms and legs. This will capture the baby's attention and develop contact and is another moment of language exposure for the baby.

- Use music and songs – hold the baby close to your body and move around the room as you sing. Your mood will transfer to her and there will be a sense of well-being and joy in this kind of contact.

- Spend time touching fingers and toes – sing or say finger rhymes like 'Eyes, nose, mouth and toes', touching or tickling to ensure that physical contact is made when language is being used.

- Put a baby on your lap facing you and spend some time rocking her or bouncing her on your knee as you have a conversation.

Toddlers

Physical contact is of prime importance to child growth and development. Children who have been denied or deprived of physical touch may crave affection and attention. Touching is an instinctive way to show care for others and children becoming friends will hold hands or put an arm around each other's shoulders. When a child receives a physical rebuff from another he becomes very upset and rejected.

In a setting the children are usually of the same age and stage of development so they do not have older role models. Consequently some children need to be shown or helped to initiate a friendly advance towards their peers. Adults may need to act as a link to help children engage with each other, perhaps suggesting that Tom would like to share in the 'tea party' or build with the blocks. Sometimes when a child is trying to communicate with another, he will do it in a physically inappropriate way such as hitting. Wrap your arms around him gently and say 'No hitting', then show him how to initiate a friendlier approach.

Practical activities

● Provide an activity such as finger painting or corn flour play where a group of children can enjoy the messy tactile sensations together.

● Make a circle by holding hands and play the game 'Ring a ring o' roses'.

● Make a cosy area where you can snuggle up and share a book with a small group.

● Rock in pairs to music, with legs crossed and arms joined. Move towards and away from each other. Sing 'Row, row, row your boat'.

● Encourage caregiving games through role play, for example hospital play (bandaging and taking care), mummies, daddies and babies (feeding, bathing and putting to bed).

● Introduce the idea of press and response using technology, for example a travel agents with a phone, a computer and a holiday video. Encourage the children to talk about holidays, take bookings and pack suitcases.

Outcomes for the child

● Physical closeness is a time for making sounds and saying words.

● Physical skills are gestures and body language is a powerful tool.

● Children learn appropriate ways to contact and touch others.

Focus points

Robert Winston, in *The Human Mind* (2004), suggests that mothers instinctively hold their baby so her left ear is close to their body. This allows sounds to be processed in the right side of the brain, the part that develops earlier than the left. Massage strengthens adult–child relationships. A number of Touch Therapy programmes are now available in the UK. Search the internet or contact your local health authority for qualified instructors.

Staff discussion

- Discuss the very simple methods that babies use to make contact. What sort of gestures do we use to reinforce what we are saying? For example, we say 'Don't cry' when we cuddle or comfort a baby.

- Talk about physical skills and social contact; some team members are much better than others at this. How can the team improve their own knowledge and understanding of this?

- As we greet a child do we touch his arm and say hello or is there a space between us?

- Observe ways that children use gestures – blowing kisses, pointing, extending their arms to ask to be lifted up.

3. Making conversation

Plan opportunities for talking together in quiet places both indoors and outdoors.

(Birth to Three Matters)

Babies

Research demonstrates that babies of just a few months old move their bodies in interactional synchrony with human speech. Observations by Colwyn Trevarthen and Martin Richards established that when babies were present with just a toy and then later with a toy and their mother there were notable differences in their movements. Babies used their hands differently, the expression on their faces changed and the tone of their voices altered. Time to have personal interactions for talking should be a part of effective planning and practice.

Practical activities

● Plan for short outdoor trips as often as possible. Be aware that buggies and pushchairs that face forward hinder language exchanges. Stop and spend time looking at the environment; engage and interact through gestures such as pointing and looking at people, places and objects.

● Select a 'cosy corner' inside – a safe, quiet place with comfortable floor seating for adults and babies. Allocate a cosy time for each baby (if only for a matter of ten minutes) where you concentrate totally on one baby and have a period of high quality time. Other staff must realise this is going on and avoid interruptions or talking over the baby's head.

● Provide a 'chat room' – this is a little enclosed den, inside or out, which could be in the shape of a pop-up tent or a simple den with light, airy material to act as a cocoon in which to talk and listen together.

● Be a baby whisperer – before and after sleep time plan a few moments where you have a calm, quiet exchange with a baby. Do this every day – it will become a special time for quiet dialogue.

● Collect props for talk such as books, puppets, toy telephones and ensure they are used to assist talk if need be.

Toddlers

Once a child begins to feel confident using language, the movements that accompany speech become more pronounced: he will use specific gestures such as pointing, open palms, shaking his head; he will look at the person he is talking to and make eye contact; he will start to modify his tone, intonation and volume.

When children are outdoors some take the opportunity to 'let off steam' and engage in vigorous play while others enjoy the chance to walk beside an adult, take her hand and be close. This is an ideal time to initiate a relaxed two-way conversation.

Practical activities

- Use child-sized puppets to start discussions about everyday matters or to introduce issues about friendships or conflict resolution. The children may reply to the puppet rather than the adult who is asking the questions.

- Introduce 'walkie talkies' so that children can play games and communicate inside/outside.

- Daily story telling/reading gives children the conventions of language, its structure and patterns. Look for books that include a soft toy such as Martin Waddell's *Can't You Sleep, Little Bear?*, or Mo Willems's *Don't Let the Pigeon Drive the Bus*, which tells the story using speech bubbles. Both are published by Walker Books. Create story bags that contain items related to the story.

- Make personalised books using children's names and photos, showing them engaged in everyday activities. It provides a starting point for talk and something to take home and share with the family. Alternatively use digital cameras and put the pictures onto a computer. Encourage the children to record their own captions or dialogue.

- Arrange workshops or printed information for parents about the importance of talking to their children and give pointers on how to do it.

- Create awe and wonder boxes, attractive giftware boxes tied with ribbon, asking 'I wonder who left this here?' 'I wonder what is inside?' 'I wonder who would need this?' Use stimulating objects that appeal to children's senses, smells, sight, sound, touch (taste may be more difficult) such as a magnifying glass, shiny jewels, shells and stones, vanilla pods and spices, velvet and silk.

Outcomes for the child

- Talk times mean personal and close opportunities to form attachments.
- Talking and communicating with others develops well-being.
- Improved confidence.
- Sharing thoughts, ideas and feelings.
- Learning about the patterns of language and conversations.

Focus points

Outside time provides good opportunities for an adult to play alongside or join in as a partner where children can enjoy sharing ideas and comments in a relaxed way. It is important that the adult questions sparingly and does not 'interrogate' children. Language needs to take place in context, where shared exchanges are meaningful, and not in a vacuum. Current research shows that a very high percentage of children enter school with poor speaking and listening skills.

Consider the children who have English as a second language. Understanding and valuing children's backgrounds is important. The key person attached to these children should learn key words and simple rhymes from that language in order to support and develop further communication.

Staff discussion

- Baby room activities have to be fairly fluid to fit around the needs of the child; however, ask staff to try to ensure that there are cosy moments and cuddle times where language is the focus.

- Including these in the information to parents is essential. Parents will see that language and communication, as well as finger printing or sand play, is playing an important part in the setting's overall ethos.

4. Getting noticed

Young babies are sociable from birth, using a variety of ways to gain attention.

(*Birth to Three Matters*)

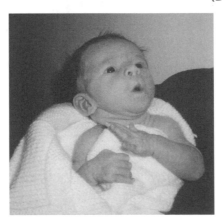

Babies

Gaining attention for a baby ranges from crying to a simple smile or banging and dropping toys in order to engage you and keep you interested. Babies may not have speech to assist them; however, they have other strategies that can be equally powerful. Listening to the pitches and style of their cries tells you whether they are hungry or very distressed, or simply saying 'I am here'. Within her first six months a baby's attention span is extremely short and she can easily be distracted. However, at the end of her ninth month of life, the very beginnings of being able to use more than one sense at a time evolves. Attention spans relate to the development of short- and long-term memory.

Practical activities

- Provide some short-handled spoons of various materials and some bowls, saucepans, or a wok so babies can bang and make noises for you to hear and get your attention!

- Collect different kinds of play telephones with different ring tones on them and play with them together. Look surprised when the phone rings and stop and respond.

- Water play using a low level tray allows babies to pat and splash to get your attention – this shows them another kind of cause and effect.

- Make a collection of different keys on key rings or a collection of small measuring spoons and let them hold and let them go.

- Use small household cylinders which they can hold and put various different items in these such as lentils or coins. Seal them carefully so that they are safe. Have several so they can find the one that gets their attention and yours!

Toddlers

Toddlers develop attention-seeking strategies such as being disruptive, being rude, challenging, and constantly interrupting. Some children are not able to articulate what is bothering them and use non-verbal ways to gain attention, for example clinging, touching or getting close. This form of attention seeking may be a sign of low self-esteem or insecurity or that the toddler has not yet established his self-image and needs reassurance. However, in some severe cases a child may seek ways to avoid being noticed and become withdrawn. As a result his social development may be delayed. It is important for the practitioner to look at the possible reasons why a child is seeking attention or otherwise.

Practical activities

- Encourage the children to be performers. Create a TV screen using a large cardboard box so that the children can act out favourite TV characters or situations. Introduce a microphone and/or karaoke machine so that they can be a 'pop idol'.

- Provide a variety of physical activities where the more robust and vigorous children can let go of steam, for example pounding dough, hammering wood, running, climbing and digging.

- Acknowledge a child's calls for attention. If the timing is inappropriate, explain why and promise that you will talk later, making sure you do! Catch attention-seeking children behaving well and praise them.

- Tell David McKee's story *Not Now, Bernard* and talk about their feelings. Ask if the monster is real, let them make up voices for the different characters and join in with the catch phrase. Contrast with Jill Murphy's *Peace at Last.*

Outcomes for the child

- Gaining attention is part of socialisation and conversation.
- Extend the range of resources beyond their own voice – using tools to get attention is useful too.
- Learning appropriate behaviour.

Focus points

There are different levels of attention seeking and we need to achieve the balance between independence and interdependence. Do all babies seek attention, and if they do not demonstrate this by about nine months such as shouting to attract your attention, imitating sounds or babbling, what actions should we take if any? Be careful not to label a child as that can become a self-fulfilling prophecy. Get to know each child's strengths and support them, praise them. Offer contact and comfort when they need it.

Staff discussion

- Ask key workers to observe and note what each of their babies do to attract attention. Do they imitate each other in a room?
- Discuss with staff the normal attention spans of babies and toddlers. What do

they know about this professionally? Parents may ask for a comment or reassurance on this; are all members of the team fully informed about this?

- Are we aware that a child who is seeking attention may have issues that are bothering him? Do we allow our own prejudices to stop us dealing with them? Do we feel that the child is trying to manipulate us, get his own way, or do we simply find him irritating?
- Observe attention-seeking children; record the frequency of interruptions, disruptive behaviour, long faces, etc. If concerned, seek external support.

5. Being together

Plan for a key person to sit with individuals or their group, focusing on different ways of communicating ... help young babies to enjoy being together and communicating with their key person.

(*Birth to Three Matters*)

Babies

Significant relationships, apart from those of the parents or carers, have an impact on the development of a child in terms of his ability to socialise and communicate. Good positive relationships engender a positive disposition to learn and partake in 'conversations'. The key person/minder provides the child with basic human needs such as nappy changing, feeding and emotional support. These, if used well, ensure that babies feel safe and secure in the company of others while being fed or changed. 'Being together' gives them positive experiences which in turn allow them to develop their confidence in communicating with others.

Practical activities

- Above the changing area have laminated photographs of faces in black and white; have some fixed on the wall close to the baby's eye line.

- Collect some photographs and trim them down to the same size; laminate them and punch a hole in the set and put them on a key ring. In this set include pictures of parents, key person, siblings – special and specific people who the child likes being together with.

- Babies have friends or certain babies they appear to be attracted to. When these special moments occur capture them using a digital camera and set up a 'being together' photo gallery on a wall or in a photograph album.

Toddlers

Early relationships can affect a person's expectation throughout his life. One of the basic foundations of human relationships is trust. For a toddler it can be an emotional learning curve to trust people outside of the family. In addition a child needs to develop a sense of self, be able to make choices and learn to do things independently. As he grows he will begin to show that he understands others' feelings, through developing empathy, maybe when he recognises another child is sad or hurt and he offers his hand or pats him gently. He will give care and attention to a younger sibling.

Practical activities

- Play board games alongside a small group of two or three children. Help them to understand the need for rules and how to play fairly.

- Help children to develop self-confidence by noting and praising their successful accomplishments and any attempt to show good social skills, such as sharing, playing fairly or waiting their turn. Strengthen this by noting the examples in a daily diary to parents, outlining the positive attributes their child is developing and how well he is behaving.

- Join in with children's activities; laugh and have fun with funny foam, corn flour mess, tossing a ball on a silk scarf. Stay relaxed and calm, engage and smile.

- Play circle games and sing songs such as 'Pop goes the weasel' or 'Here we go round the mulberry bush'.

- Encourage more reticent children to help you with simple tasks – returning resources, setting out snacks or washing dolls on a one-to-one basis.

Outcomes for the child

- The development of a close relationship with a key person/minder helps to promote the child's feeling of well-being.
- Being together has many advantages and is part of development.
- Social skills develop and friendships are formed.
- Self-confidence increases.

Focus points

It is important to consider the criteria for assigning a key person to a child and what steps would need to be taken if the dynamics of a paired relationship are not working. Peer friendships are often formed through a common schema and this may influence the choice of play mates. Friendships are fluid and may not always be happy; some will eventually end in tears and sadness. Those children who have developed good social skills, such as being friendly when joining in and not being aggressive or taking over the play, are often more popular.

Staff discussion

- Ask staff to think carefully about their key group and if there are any children in it they find difficult to bond with. Why is this?
- Ask staff to plan thoughtfully when they have key person time – do they evaluate this time honestly and ever make action plans to improve it? Talk about the outcomes for the children if you have a key person system and ensure all staff know these.
- Some children have difficulties in relating to others for many different reasons. Observe, track and record children's relationships with others. Be aware that if you feel a child has serious difficulties relating to other children/adults, you may need to seek external support and advice.

6. Positive communication

Ensure there is good communication between parents and practitioners to provide babies and children with positive models.

(Birth to Three Matters)

Babies

Babies sense harmony and so it is important that those caring for them emit positive feelings towards each other. Babies feel better about their carers and tend to learn faster if they feel attachment. Where there are multiple attachments (when they are in day care or with a childminder) the relationship between those sharing those attachments is very important. The baby needs to feel safe and secure and any negativity in attitudes does not support the child overall.

Greeting and saying farewell are important communication moments. Babies learn to wave their hands very early on. Communication between the parent and practitioner at this time is important. Body language as well as spoken language plays an important part in this relationship too.

Practical activities

- Have a hello and goodbye moment – focus first on the baby and then follow this by saying 'hello' to her parent or carer. Teach some simple waving songs and activities and share them with parents so they can do them at home to ensure continuity.

- Ensure there are a collection of songs/stories with Mummy and Daddy mentioned in them. Have photographs of the baby with key persons and parents for the baby to look at – this visual representation can be useful.

- Birthdays are special days and if you have the child that day make a simple diary of their day and take photographs to ensure parents feel part of that day too. Being an effective communicator yourself is the best possible role model for the baby and parent.
- Make a family (Mummy, Daddy and baby) using teddy bears. Provide simple role-play resources such as hats or cups to play with. This role playing of relationships is important.

Toddlers

Young children learn how the wider world will interact with them through the way their own families work. Sometimes a toddler arrives in the setting with a ready-made role of being the joker, the clown, the carer or the victim within his family group and will continue with that role. Young children model themselves on significant adults and this can be negative as well as positive. For a practitioner it is essential to help children understand who they are and to provide them with a positive role model – someone who is warm, responsive, genuine yet firm and fair.

Practical activities

- Understand home cultures. Take time to have a dialogue with parents to establish how simple boundaries and rules are implemented at home. Find out if there are any gender roles that are culturally specific, for example expectations for women, male hierarchy, and the role of grandparents. Ensure you know and understand religious issues, food, special days, events and celebrations. Observe how families greet each other, take leave of each other and comfort each other. How close do they get to each other?
- Ask parents to provide photos or videos of life at home, holidays, excursions, celebrations that they would like to share with the setting.
- Develop activities that reflect their family life, holidays and recreation, cooking and musical tastes. Encourage parents to supply photographs, materials, utensils and objects that are familiar and enjoyed by the children.
- Avoid using stereotypical phrases such as 'Big boys don't cry' or passing comments on unfamiliar food or clothing.
- Tell the story of *The Most Beautiful Child* by William Papas. Explore and respect the diversity in appearance and concentrate on opportunities to stress similarities and appreciate differences. For example, we may have hair that is long, short, straight or curly; some children may be bald as a result of an

illness. Talk about how our hair has changed since being a baby or how at times we wear our hair differently. Collect adverts showing a variety of styles and ask for their comments.

- Develop and support with appropriate resources role-play scenarios that echo family life – births, marriages, funerals, religious celebrations, birthdays, hospitals. Join in and play alongside, responding to any questions and conversations that result.

Outcomes for the child

- Feeling reassured by a seamless exchange of carers.
- Seeing and hearing positive relationships between adults.
- Consistency in communication.
- The development of opportunities for open and honest communication.
- An understanding of others.

Focus points

It is crucial that staff, and key persons in particular, take time to develop good knowledge and understanding of a child, his family and background. Having a positive reciprocal relationship with parents that includes mutual respect, co-operation and commitment will be beneficial to all concerned. Staff need to appreciate that there are many varied types of parenting, cultural rules and roles. It is vitally important that staff remain non-judgemental and avoid stereotyping families that appear to differ from the norm. We are individuals and so different techniques and approaches will be required to ensure that the quality of relationships and communication is good.

Staff discussion

- During a staff meeting show colleagues through example how it feels to be greeted and smiled at, or how you can use body language to be very negative. Talk about this and present some anonymous observations – pull out the positive points from these and have staff draw up ten simple points that they agree to follow.
- Look at the quality of written communication you provide for parents and the wider community. Are there ways this can be improved? Are you taking into consideration the needs of all the parents within your group?
- Review your Equal Opportunities policy and make sure that it is implemented in everyday practice.

References

Bowlby, J. (1953) *Child Care and the Growth of Love.* London: Penguin.

Christian, L. G. (2006) 'Understanding families: Applying family systems theory to early childhood practice', *Young Children*, 61 (1): 12–20. Available at www.journal.naeyc.org

DfES (Department for Education and Skills) (2002) *Birth to Three Matters: A Framework to Support Children in their Earliest Years.* London: DfES.

DfES (Department for Education and Skills) (2003) *Every Child Matters.* London: DfES.

DfES (Department for Education and Skills) (2005) *Communicating Matters: The Strands of Communication and Language.* London: DfES

DfES (Department for Education and Skills)/DWP (Department for Work and Pensions) (2003) *National Standards for Under 8s Day Care and Childminding (Full Day Care).* London: DfES.

McKee, D. (1996) *Not Now, Bernard.* London: Red Fox.

Murphy, J. (1995) *Peace at Last.* London: Macmillan Children's Books.

Papas, W. (1973) *The Most Beautiful Child.* Oxford: Oxford University Press.

QCA (Qualifications and Curriculum Authority) (2000) *Curriculum Guidance for the Foundation Stage.* London: QCA.

Schaffer, H. R. and Emerson, P. F. (1964) 'The development of social attachments in infancy', *Monographs of the Society for Research in Child Development*, 29 (Series No. 94).

Waddell, M. (2000) *Can't You Sleep, Little Bear?* London: Walker Books.

Willems, M. (2004) *Don't Let the Pigeon Drive the Bus.* London: Walker Books.

Winston, R. (2004) *The Human Mind: And How to Make the Most of It.* London: Bantam.

Resources

The Basic Skills Agency provides booklets for parents about talking with babies and toddlers.

The National Literacy Trust *Talk to Your Baby* campaign pages – www.literacytrust.org.uk/talktoyourbaby/index.html

2 Finding a voice

Introduction

Language distinguishes us from the rest of creation. The importance of the sounds and babbling of a young baby should not be underestimated as these form the first steps along the road to 'finding a voice'. The developments that lead children to become confident and competent language users are unique and important as they connect directly with a child's intellectual development.

For this reason it is important that we understand the stages a child goes through in terms of this development and tailor our educational strategies accordingly. For example, it is now known that rote or repetitive teaching does not bring about understanding and the use of this technique with young children is inappropriate. Similarly, it is important for carers to recognise the different communication problems children may experience, such as a child withdrawing his use of communication when he is distressed or anxious.

By familiarising themselves with the developmental stages of babies and toddlers, carers can equip themselves to support children in their development of vital communication skills. However, whilst it is useful to recognise the existence of developmental stages, it is also important that carers remember that each child is an individual and that expectations must be reasonable and well informed.

By using routines as well as play, carers can provide opportunities for children and toddlers to interact and engage as active listeners. Provision of well-chosen resources can support children, encourage and enthuse them to communicate, express, represent, question and predict using their own voices.

Giving children the skills to communicate well is essential as they will use these skills to socialise, express feelings about themselves and others and to discover and investigate their world. The confidence this instills brings with it positive results both in terms of the children's disposition and their general state of well-being.

1. The impulse to communicate

Young babies communicate in a variety of ways including crying, gurgling, babbling and squealing.

(*Birth to Three Matters*)

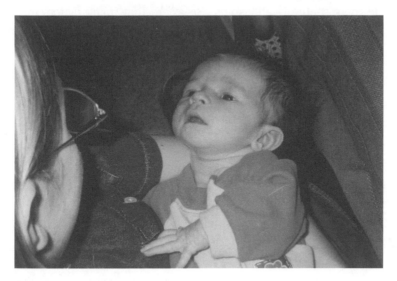

Babies

Babies communicate with their body language as well as using language sounds. Communication is usually only partially oral. The sound and tone a baby uses alongside her facial expressions are only part of her communication strategies. Babies combine their body posture and gestures to 'communicate' a great deal. Newborns use crying as their main method of communication.

Practical activities

- Hold baby close and look her in the eye, speaking softly so she hears your voice. Do this as often as possible to establish closeness and communication as babies are social beings too.

- Use feeding times as an opportunity to talk with the baby again as baby is close at this time, and will enjoy hearing your voice.

- Use changing nappies as another time to talk and chatter to babies. This will reassure them and while they are lying down you can make eye contact.

- Babies respond to singing – it doesn't matter if you think you cannot sing at all! Use singing and humming with your baby to communicate sounds.

- Make a recording of the sounds that babies make and listen to it. Are there any sounds that are more frequent than others?

Toddlers

As toddlers grow in confidence and are able to communicate clearly they develop ownership and control over their lives. It is suggested that those children who have the impulse to communicate, who can express their feelings and their needs, are able to build more secure relationships. Be aware that many factors may inhibit the impulse to talk: the time of day, the noise level within the room, if they are hungry or tired and also if they are feeling rushed.

Practical activities

- Provide a variety of real, concrete activities that encourage co-operation and sharing.

- Help the children to learn words that name and describe their feelings. Use photographs, puppets and stories, and encourage the children to talk about them. In this way they will begin to recognise their physical feelings and their emotional feelings and those of others. Observe if they can differentiate the feeling of falling over and hurting their knee with the feeling of being left out of a group. Ask them to talk about the things they like to cuddle when they feel upset.

- Encourage children to describe their paintings and mark making. Often they can think faster than they can talk so be patient and give them time to formulate what they want to say.

- Set up the role-play corner with a range of old telephones, mobile phones and voice recorders. Initiate play by presenting a problem, for example you are expecting a visitor for tea and she hasn't arrived. How can you find out if she is still coming?

Outcomes for the child

- Babies and toddlers feel respected, that they are listened to and can communicate to each other and their carers.
- Communication is used to convey the needs of a child.
- Children begin to be aware of their own feelings and those of others.

Focus points

All practitioners, whether they work with babies or toddlers, are teachers of communication and language. In order to support children's development as effective communicators, practitioners need to ensure they have daily interactions with each child. Being a reflective practitioner means thinking about the quality of even the briefest moments of communication that are shared with a child.

Children who find it difficult to talk and express their feelings and frustrations may resort to whining, crying and even hitting out. The impulse to communicate and interact with others helps children to develop friendships.

Staff discussion

- Get staff to talk about body language and how children use this to convey meaning – discuss communication in a much wider sense.
- Photograph significant moments and use paper speech bubbles to record what the baby/toddler was trying to convey at that time – this will need to be jotted down when the picture is taken. Fix in a photograph album, their record book or on a pin board.

2. Responding to sounds

Note the wide variety of sounds a young baby produces and how adults try to understand and respond to them.

(Birth to Three Matters)

Babies

Babies listen to sounds in the womb before they are born. After birth their hearing is acute and gets better; they become increasingly aware of the distinction between different kinds of sounds, especially between linguistic and other sounds. When being nursed they enjoy the sound and feel of the heartbeat. Babies' babbling can sound like little sentences in a foreign language; however, you may be able to notice different rhythms, tones and stress patterns. Babbling does indicate there is a form of readiness of the nervous system as it prepares for speech.

Practical activities

- Greetings such as 'hello' and 'goodbye' are very important and these are often accompanied by waving or gestures. Echoing any sounds or imitating the gestures that babies use supports and acknowledges these key moments of meeting or leaving.

- Scanning and focusing on sounds has not been fully developed so when a sound is heard, pointing, saying what it is or showing an object supports babies as they begin to scan their auditory surroundings.

- Make a 'Sound treasure basket' – a soft wicker basket full of items that make sounds – and explore with your baby. Observe and note which sounds get more of a response than others. Listen to the sounds babies make when they hear sounds.

- Shake rattles when you play with babies as this begins to develop 'foreground' sounds.

Toddlers

Music and sounds develop a sense of rhythm that is fundamental to language development. Activities that encourage children to identify different sounds help to train the ear to recognise pitch and fine tune the auditory system. Traditional songs and rhymes have a distinct rhythm, often repeating phrases and this also helps to establish memory. Sound is closely linked to our physical movement. The auditory nerve connects with all the muscles in the body. Sounds are vibrations in the ear and the ear controls our sense of balance, which is vital to our movement.

Practical activities

- Play 'Hide and seek' using a sound to locate an object. As they get nearer, the sound gets louder.

- Make a rain box. Seal fine sand securely in a tin. Gently tip it and listen to the noises that resemble the sound of the rain, or waves on a sea-shore. Using different grades of sand or gravel will change the sound.

- Create a Lotto game with the children's photos and their names. When you say their name they place a counter on their board.

- Make a kitchen band. Use metal pots and pans and wooden spoons. This helps to develop pitch and tone. Ensure that some of the pots produce high notes and some low. Encourage the children to create soft as well as loud sounds.

- Fill different containers such as flower pots or plastic bottles with buttons, coins, rice and dried beans. Listen to the sound produced. Hide the bottles behind a screen and see if they can identify which one it is. Start with three distinct sounds and then increase to more subtle differences.

  Caution: Ensure that all the bottle caps are firmly secured so that small items cannot fall out and be swallowed.

- Encourage the children to be very quiet and focus their attention on listening to the small sounds around them: a tap dripping, a clock ticking.

Outcomes for the child

- Babies and toddlers use sounds to communicate their needs and wants.

- Making sounds supports pathways to the later acquisition of auditory and verbal skills and the lack of sound making raises awareness as a possible indicator of language delay.

- The children will begin to distinguish differences in pitch, tone and volume.

Focus points

Focus on the sounds in the environment – think about the sounds babies come into contact with. Taping and noting sounds over time, map how a child uses his own sounds, knows and recognises certain sounds and is distressed when he hears loud, unknown sounds. Children need to be able to discriminate between sounds so it is important to help them focus their listening skills.

Staff discussion

● Observe the times that babies make the most sound and what sounds they use to demonstrate they are enjoying an activity. Discuss how adults recognise babies' different levels of crying to get attention or to show distress.

● How do staff use parent/carer information on what sounds babies use at home?

● Go through your story books, songs and rhymes; list those that feature sounds.

● Use the internet to find stories with sound tracks.

3. Creating sounds

Encourage exploration and imitation of sound by providing... everyday objects found in the home.

(*Birth to Three Matters*)

Babies

Babies can make conversations with sounds. Allowing a baby to have time to assimilate and imitate is essential. Babies have times when they are absorbed in their own sound making. Repeating sounds back to babies provides an opportunity for them to hear separate sounds. This in turn assists in the development of movements made with a baby's lips and tongue. Once babies become sitters, standers and explorers (8–18 months) it is important not just to mimic sounds but to introduce words to go with actions. Resources are very useful with this task.

Practical activities

- Have a collection of board or fabric books with sounds. Spend time sharing these and listening to the sounds.

- Use weaved wicker balls and place bells inside them so they can be rolled and listened to.

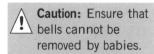
Caution: Ensure that bells cannot be removed by babies.

- Investigate some *unused* soft pet toys. Many have squeaky sounds in them and can provide an additional set of resources.

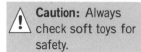
Caution: Always check soft toys for safety.

- Have a collection of 'squeaky' toys mixed up with other toys and encourage the babies to explore the collection to find the sound toys.

- Investigate activity mats and find some that have good integrated sound elements.

- Have mirrors all around the setting – some in the cot (there are special ones), near the nappy change area and on the wall so babies can see themselves and their facial features as they explore the sounds they make.

Toddlers

Being able to differentiate sounds and imitate them are the prerequisites for language, speaking and listening.

Practical activities

- Encourage the children to clap and walk to the beat while singing a familiar song.

- Provide the children with objects that make sounds or simple musical instruments. Ask them to make both long and short sounds – have a long snake and a short one to show which sound to make. Use a big teddy and a small teddy to indicate loud or soft sounds.

- Identify characters in a story by the way that they speak, for example 'Three Billy Goats Gruff' or the wolf in 'Little Red Riding Hood'.

- Play a sound version of 'Blind Man's Bluff' where the children try to locate the sound of each other's voices and say who it is.

- Play 'Hide and seek' – one child is asked to find a hidden object while the others make loud sounds when he is 'warm' and soft sounds when he is 'cold'.

- Use a musical signal to show when activities end or transition times occur.

- Collect objects that make a sound and put them into different categories: those that make sounds by hitting, plucking, shaking, blowing; or those that make high pitched, low, soft, sharp or deep sounds. Encourage the children to combine different sounds and make sounds that ring, bang or thud.
- Listen to sounds within the environment; find those that are repetitive, constant or unusual.

Outcomes for the child

- Some sounds give pleasure and support emotional well-being.
- Understanding and experiencing the extremes of sound: loud and soft, long or short.

Focus points

Focusing on exploration and imitation may require more creative resourcing. Household items encourage sound exploration as much as expensive toys, for example wooden spoons, saucepans, plastic bottles that are sealed securely and contain coins, buttons, dried beans or rice.

Music is a basic human need; we are musical beings and respond to the rhythms of our bodies: pulse, heartbeat and the rhythms of our environment. However, young children's pulses are much faster than adults' and their walking may not always match the beat. Any musical experience should be enjoyable and appropriate for their level. Look for songs that have repetitive phrases such as 'Skip to my loo' or 'This old man'. The younger the child the more natural, spontaneous and unstructured the experience should be.

Staff discussion

- Ask staff to make a sound trail or a sound rail, for example saucepan lids hung on a line and hit with a wooden spoon. Have different items for the babies and one for the toddlers; discuss the differences.
- Ask staff to do an audit of the equipment that could be used to develop sound awareness.
- Discuss the use of music or musical instruments. What is the effect of music and is it used appropriately for babies and toddlers – is it too loud at times for some?

- Babies need music too. Not only does it give them pleasure but it improves their ability to concentrate. Investigate the research in relation to babies and toddlers exposed to classical music, Mozart in particular.

4. Using words

Young children use single word and two word utterances to convey simple and more complex messages.

(Birth to Three Matters)

Babies

All babies are unique. Baby babble – the experimentation with sounds – is important. The front of the mouth is where the sounds such as *p* and *b* are produced, the middle mouth is where *t* and *d* are made and the back of the mouth is for *k* and *g*. Babies may produce words at around 12 months but some may take much longer; it does not necessarily mean there is a speech problem. The sounds contained in babble support the first words such as 'dada' or 'mama'. Interestingly the names for parents are quite similar in many languages. The correlation of the spoken word and the understanding a baby has of language does not match: the baby may say three words but understand fifty. It is easier to start focusing on words of one syllable.

Practical activities

- Have a repertoire of simple songs and rhymes which you say while you bounce the baby on your knees. This gives a sense of rhyme and timing to the words. Include nonsense words and sounds.

- Instead of singing a song try saying the same words in different ways – whispered, soft, loud and high pitched.

- Play 'Where is the sound?' – take a wind-up toy, whether it be musical or just a sound, and hide it. Ask the baby where has it gone. Hide it under a cushion or cloth or inside a box.

- Use books as a stimulus. Ask them to recall the story through the use of open questioning such as 'Who knows what the gingerbread man said?'

- Start naming and labelling familiar items to encourage the development of vocabulary.

- During mealtimes use simple descriptive sound words like 'yum yum' to express pleasant emotions. Relate single words or two-word phrases to routines. In this way routines are used to convey messages.

Toddlers

During the toddler years words start to become real human exchanges and the child gains more control in his life, although in these early stages sentences are shortened versions such as 'me go play'. For language to have meaning and be at the centre of children's learning it needs to be linked to real experiences. It becomes a tool for discussing their ideas and their plans, helping them to think things through and to talk about their feelings.

Practical activities

- Look for jingles and rhymes that use explosive sounds such as 'Five fat peas in the pot' to develop speech muscles. Blow feathers across a table or burst bubbles and say 'Pop'. Blow paint through a straw to make colourful patterns.

- Use a mirror and pull funny faces as you over-exaggerate the vowel sounds and strengthen the lips. Open wide and say 'aah'. Stretch the lips tightly to play with the sound 'eee' or really round 'OOOOh'. Pretend you have sticky paper on the back of your top front teeth and use your tongue 'ttt' to get it off.

- Play games such as 'Head, shoulders, knees and toes' as you name and touch the correct body parts.

- Encourage the children to follow simple instructions and develop their auditory memory, for example 'Put the spoon into the cup'. Gradually increase the complexity to 'Put the spoon into the blue cup' or 'the big blue cup'.

- Record simple instructions for games or activities onto a tape recorder. Repeat them clearly and give instructions on when to turn off the recorder.

- Use simple visual cues to encourage the children to look and listen.
- Photograph the children engaged in an activity and then display in a simple sequence. Encourage them to recall what they were doing.

Outcomes for the child

- Using babbling as a springboard to simple early single-word speech.
- Repeating words in various daily routines enables young children to listen, understand and use words themselves.
- Being able to convey meaning using word utterances to communicate simple messages.
- Understanding that language carries meaning and following simple instructions.

Focus points

Listening to babies babbling is a useful observation and can help to identify the stages of language development. Experiment using music as a way to concentrate on sound as this helps to support brain development. Adults need to ensure that when they want to gain a child's attention they use his name, face him, make eye contact and speak clearly.

Developing auditory memory is crucial for language development, and activities that encourage this help to develop the correct pathways in the brain.

Staff discussion

- Focus and record the development of the sounds used by a baby when babbling to the first words spoken. Encourage staff to use tapes to record spoken sounds (in the baby area) and speech in the toddler room. It will be necessary to add an observation too and even photographs so that they can capture the gesture and mood of the observation.
- Observe children using sounds to accompany movement, such as pushing a train and uttering 'choo, choo'.
- Look for ways to build up this tool for talking toddlers by helping them to develop clear speech. This can be achieved by performing simple exercises involving muscles in the lips, the tongue and the mouth. Chewy foods and finger snacks also help.

5. Becoming confident

Being a confident and competent language user . . . the impulse to communicate.

(Birth to Three Matters)

Babies

The impulse to communicate with others is very much based on the likelihood of response. If a baby finds that the simplest form of communication is acknowledged and respected, then this will give her the self-esteem and confidence to play with language. Encouraging this 'can do' spirit is very important both at home and in the setting. Babies do have voices for us to hear from their moment of birth; they may have small voices but they have powerful messages. They have the impulse to communicate and need a response to make it feel purposeful. A baby may find her voice but it is worthless if it is not listened to!

Practical activities

● Provide a 'feelings treasure basket' (a wicker basket filled with objects). Include items that are soft and you can say 'Ahhh' with or objects that tickle to make babies smile and giggle.

● Provide some draw-string bags or simple boxes with surprises in so that the baby will show awe and wonder and to encourage an impulse to respond.

● Going outside with babies introduces them to new sights and sounds.

● Observe their expressions and responses when a bird flies away and then returns fairly quickly.

- Using pop-up toys and simple puppets that are based on the element of surprise generates an impulsive response – ensure that some of these are in the toy collections you have.
- Books with flaps or pop ups introduce change and surprises – add these into your collection of baby books.

Toddlers

Toddlers begin to develop both confidence and competence with their language skills; however, these can be developed further by sensitive adults. They can initiate interactions and encourage the more reticent child to contribute. Non-threatening activities such as pretend play allow a child to explore ideas, think out loud and at times experience a fearful situation, such as the chant 'Fee Fi Fo Fum' of the giant in 'Jack and the Beanstalk', in a safe environment.

Practical activities

- Discuss with the group the activities that are available and ask the children to plan what they intend to do during the session. Later on ask them to tell you what they did, reflecting with them.
- Set up co-operative play situations that encourage social interactions such as scenarios in pretend play. Have a good range of resources to allow children to become a character. Design activities that relate to their own experiences such as shopping for shoes, going to the hairdressers or the car wash, or exciting scenarios such as 'being' firemen.
- Introduce a range of resources from other cultures in order to spark questions and introduce descriptive language. Have a collection of interesting items to explore, for example old clocks and their working parts, information and technology (IT) equipment.
- Encourage the children to tell stories to the group. This may start off as a one liner, such as 'I went out', but gradually as they grow in confidence their story will develop.
- Read or tell a story, pausing to ask what they think will happen. Encourage the children to 'read' the story, remembering the events.
- Provide a mysterious large cardboard box and ask 'What do you think is inside?'

Outcomes for the child

- Feeling that they have a voice and it is listened to.
- Using their voice to express their needs and feelings.
- Understanding that a voice can be a gesture and also a sign.
- Raised confidence.
- Clarification of ideas.

Focus points

The impulse to communicate arises from the balance of feeling secure and safe and being given stimulating, exciting opportunities. Daily routines help the children to feel secure. When adults listen attentively, they can more effectively meet the needs and interests of the children in their care and, in addition, they can get to know the children really well. Finding time to listen to children should be planned so that the children are not hurried, adults are not stressed and talk is conversational rather than managerial.

Staff discussion

- Ask staff to note when they feel babies use their voices most. Are they surprised with some of the impulsive responses babies make?
- Observe a colleague as she interacts with a baby on the floor or with a toddler engaged in an activity. Focus on the language used, her vocabulary and ideas, or the sounds, gestures and movements that the child makes.
- Be aware of who you talk to and interact with. Do you give all children an equal chance to communicate or just those who are most articulate or seek attention?

6. Exploring and experimenting

Sharing the fun of discovery and valuing babies' 'words'; e.g. by bringing the doll in response to 'baba'.

(Birth to Three Matters)

Babies

The first early words are important and supporting and extending this newfound skill of using a word is crucial. Some of a baby's early speech is often understood by the family and significant adults such as her key person. As babies start to discover new words and begin to communicate, recognition of their efforts is vital. *Birth to Three Matters* reinforces the importance of having a key person under the section on effective practice. The fun of using other words such as 'Uh-oh' when something has been dropped also plays a part of this newly found verbal skill.

Practical activities

● Some babies favour cats, dogs, faces and certain objects and identify them by the sound they make. If a child is showing this as an interest, collect lots of pictures and put them in a small photo album which you can look through and share together.

● Provide simple, imaginative play things such as soft dolls and pieces of cloth so that the dolly can be like a baby and be put to bed or have a bottle. This encourages language reinforcement opportunities.

● Have a collection of the same item, for example different balls in a basket, and explore the balls – saying 'Where is the ball?' and repeating the word 'ball' so that the baby can see, hear and feel the object and associate the word with it too.

- Introduce questions like 'Where has it gone?' – it is important that young children hear this kind of language. It also gives them opportunities to interact. Remember though: be ready for the 'Why?' stage of development where you have to be prepared to answer them!

Toddlers

The English language is made up of 26 letters and 43 sounds (*c* and *k* sound the same). These sounds are combined in many ways to form words. Young children and toddlers discover the fun of making words and communicating their ideas. They need self-confidence and persistence to keep on trying, sometimes making mistakes and often repeating words. Children understand much more of the language than they use.

Practical activities

- Play the game 'I went shopping and I bought...' This helps to develop children's memory and auditory sequencing skills.

- Provide a tray with objects on. Show the objects and as you point to each one name it. Cover the tray and ask them to recall an object. Later ask a child to select one of the objects when given a simple description, for example 'Find me the big red ball, please'. Combine this with an 'I spy' game.

- Play a movement game to introduce the following words: 'on', 'in', 'under', 'on top'. Jump in the hoop, out of the hoop and so on.

- Have a variety of pictures of animals or toy animals, such as a dog, a hamster, a cat, a pig. Include two or three different pictures of the same animal. Ask the children to group them so they match the picture to the spoken word. Ask 'What is this?' 'Let's put all the dogs here'.

Outcomes for the child

- Developing confidence with sounds and words.
- Finding out that playing with language can be fun.
- Being able to communicate with others through sounds or words as well as gestures and body language.
- Learning to group and classify objects.
- Discovering rules of language.
- Developing auditory memory.

Focus points

Children understand much more language than they use. To remember something we need to register it, give it attention and then enjoy opportunities for lots of repetition. Children need to be shown how to look carefully and really concentrate as this is one of the first steps to developing a good memory. Listening requires the development of specific auditory skills: discrimination between sounds, connecting and linking through association, memory and sequencing. Toddlers begin to use joining words or conjunctions such as 'and', 'so', 'because', giving more meaning to their spoken language.

It is not always necessary to correct a toddler's 'mistakes' (I goed, I comed) especially if it stops the language flow. These mistakes show that a child has understood the rules of grammar but not the exceptions. However, adults can help to extend the child's language by echoing with the correct form: *child*: 'Daddy home'; *adult*: 'Yes, Daddy is coming home'.

Staff discussion

- Observe and record when babies begin to use words and share these special moments with parents. Decide how you will do this as a team.
- Listen to children and note the main key words being used by a group.
- Look for different ways for children to communicate such as painting, dancing, modelling and imagining.
- Talk with parents and find out the words used at home for meals, bedtime and toileting. Some languages do not use all the same sounds as in English. Be aware of second language children and the implications it may have when they start to make sounds and say words.

References

DfES (Department for Education and Skills) (2002) *Birth to Three Matters: A Framework to Support Children in their Earliest Years*. London: DfES.

DfES (Department for Education and Skills) (2003) *Every Child Matters*. London: DfES.

DfES (Department for Education and Skills)/DWP (Department for Work and Pensions) (2003) *National Standards for Under 8s Day Care and Childminding (Full Day Care)*. London: DfES.

3 Listening and responding

Introduction

In order to communicate with each other we use a code that has a system of rules that we learn to understand. It allows us to share our thoughts and ideas and lets others know our individual needs and our wants. Initially babies and young children begin to make meaning of the language that they hear and then they begin to imitate the sounds. Communication eventually becomes a two-way interaction that is both receptive (understanding what is said) and expressive (speaking meaning).

A skilful practitioner plays a crucial part in the development of a child's early language. She needs to be able to develop warmth and empathy with the children in her care, within an environment that is secure and in which the children feel at ease. Even very young babies are aware when an adult is distracted or non-responsive and continual non-involvement can have long-term detrimental effects. Babies are keen to engage in social contact and enjoy being with other babies and young children. The key person needs to take time to appreciate babies' attempts to communicate with others and respond to them sensitively. Once a toddler attempts early conversation, practitioners need to listen attentively and patiently and explore strategies to extend their learning. The government is recognising the importance of communication and has produced guidelines for training practitioners called *Communicating Matters* (DfES, 2005).

Good professional development can ensure that practitioners keep abreast of new research and increase their knowledge and understanding of child development. The use of child observations, noting in particular where there have been significant moments of learning, and sharing these with key adults, can help to ensure that effective 'next steps' are planned for the individual child. The development of a true partnership with parents has benefits for all concerned. When practitioners have a good understanding of a child's background and family culture they are better equipped to provide for the child. If parents are aware that the caregiver has their child's interests at heart, they will become more supportive and responsive.

1. Listening and paying attention

Long before young babies can communicate verbally, they listen to, distinguish and respond to intonations in adults' voices.

(Birth to Three Matters)

All children, whatever their age, need to be talked to and listened to. Communication is a two-way process. They develop their communication skills by interpreting the messages they receive from faces, gestures, sounds and touch.

Babies

Babies start to take an interest in what's going on around them from a very early age. When lying on their front they will push themselves up to see what's happening. Interaction is vitally important for the child and rewarding for the adult. Children learn language through the repetition of facial expressions, gestures, movements and the pace and tone of your voice.

Practical activities

- Babies of six weeks old will follow faces around the room, so hold them gently and look into their eyes; speak softly, saying their name; smile, raise your eyebrows or make silly faces and stick out your tongue. Watch to see their reactions and if they mirror your expressions.

- Shake a rattle and give praise when she responds to it by smiling at her and using a gentle, positive tone of voice. Have a rattle in each hand and shake them alternately. Give one to the baby – you shake; she shakes.

- By six months she will laugh and chuckle and make a variety of sounds; copy these sounds and repeat them back to her. Record them and play them back to her. Observe if she shows any signs of recognition.

- Emphasise certain words with gestures and movement, such as 'Bye-bye' with a wave of the hand and 'Bedtime' when you settle her down. Shake your head and change your tone of voice to say 'No'.

Toddlers

Research shows that 85–95 per cent of our communication is non-verbal. From an early age a child will interpret your tone of voice, facial expression and body language and judge if the interaction is going to be positive, pleasant or negative. Make sure that your tone, face and body all give the same message or the message he receives will be confused. He recognises the importance of certain words by the strong emphasis given to them and will distinguish between praise, excitement or disapproval. During this time he may well pick up a variety of swear words and use them for effect.

Practical activities

- Use paper plate puppets to show different facial expressions such as sadness, anger or happiness. Ask the children what they think the person is saying.

- Uncover part of a picture of a face and ask what the person is saying. Start with the eyebrows and slowly reveal the rest of the face.

- Teach the uses of social language. Explore the many ways you can say the same thing but in a different tone: Hello, I'm sorry, Stop that! Well done! Can I play? Display photos or pictures to illustrate these situations and attach speech bubbles to reinforce and remind the children.

- Explore conversations in traditional stories such as 'Goldilocks'. How many ways could the bears express their disappointment that she had eaten their porridge?

- Children need to know and understand when they have done well, through your approval and genuine praise.

Outcomes for the child

- Children feel more valued.
- They begin to develop their communication skills and respond to others.
- They are learning to follow instructions and adjust their behaviour.

Focus points

It is believed that 50 per cent of the brain's development takes place during the first six months of life. It is therefore important that adults stimulate babies' communication skills by initiating interactions. Give children undivided attention to show that you are interested in what they are saying. Make eye contact and respond by nodding or asking relevant questions. Do not hurry them as they need time to think and organise their thoughts. Think about the way you ask questions – keep them simple and open. It is less intimidating if you are on the same level as the child. Be aware that children with special educational needs may not have the skills to interpret an adult's more subtle intonations. Those children who do not have English as their first language may not understand or respond to verbal cues. Sometimes a change in accent or stress on a word can cause misunderstandings.

Staff discussion

- Record your own voice when you are giving instructions or talking with children. Do you show empathy, stimulation and interest in their responses? Are there certain phrases that you use repeatedly? Do you speak in the same way to all the children?
- Children understand more than we know. Do you and your colleagues or parents ever talk over the children's heads?

2. Serious and playful responses

> . . . explore and talk about things which interest young children indoors
> and outdoors, and listen to and respond to their questions, both
> serious and playful.
>
> (*Birth to Three Matters*)

Babies

Babies respond differently to experiences meaning that a rough and tumble may
be fun for one but may terrify another. It is important to get to know the personality
and preferences of each baby in your care. The adult selects the experiences for
the baby, who does not know that a 'Peek-a-boo' game is both exciting and fun
until she has learnt to share her carer's laughter.

Practical activities

- Have fun as you touch the baby's toes and say 'This little piggy went to market',
  or 'Incy Wincy Spider' and 'Round and round the garden' while circling her
  palm and tickling her gently.

- Use soft finger puppets as you talk to her. Make the puppet dance this way and
  that; tickle her and stroke her arm with the puppet. She will be fascinated as
  she watches and may begin to babble to it.

- Play 'Peek-a-boo' at feeding or nappy-changing times, catching and diverting
  eye contact and smiling.

- For quieter moments, or to calm a distressed child, softly sing a lullaby or croon
  sounds while gently massaging her hand. Sing 'Rock-a-bye baby' when putting
  youngsters down to rest.

- Play chasing games, crawling along the floor as you say 'I am coming to get
  you!' The baby will squeal with delight and excitement. When you catch her
  give her a gentle nuzzle. She may well say 'gen' or 'more'.

Toddlers

Young children start to play with language spontaneously, and from a vocabulary of around a dozen words and simple three-word phrases their language begins to develop rapidly. They make up words, play with sounds and often repeat words they take a fancy to. They talk because they have something to say, something to share or wonder about. It is important to establish an understanding that the children are free to talk and question and that the adults are available to listen to them.

Practical activities

- Listen and observe children as they play; record their conversations and note the words they use.
- Introduce exciting toys and models such as a monster or a strange machine. Ask the children to suggest a name, for example the 'Monster muncher who mashes marshmallows'. Stimulate interest in a soft toy or a puppet by speaking in a funny voice. Leave the toy for the children to play with.
- Get to know their current favourite TV character and introduce a picture, toy or model. Encourage them to 'be' the character.
- Stimulate curiosity and questioning by introducing new items to everyday activities, for example coloured ice-cubes in the water tray. Promote discussion by asking, 'I wonder what will happen if . . . ?' Give them things to puzzle about, to discover and talk about. Listen carefully to their observations and comments and follow their lead by helping them to clarify their ideas.
- Use interactive stories such as 'Going on a lion hunt' where they can join in with movement and words.

Outcomes for the child

- Social interaction can be fun.
- Involvement in an activity gives intrinsic enjoyment and satisfaction.
- Language has a pattern and a rhythm.

Focus points

Nursery rhymes can be fun but also help children to learn the rhythm of a language. Young children enjoy fantasy, novelty and challenge so it is important to provide activities that encourage this. Having a problem and solving it promotes serious thought and reasoning while giving a good feeling of accomplishment and satisfaction. By introducing fantasy or whimsy into their role play you can allow them to freely use their imagination.

Staff discussion

- Develop a resource of nursery rhymes and use them regularly with the children. They help the children to begin to play with words and sounds and build up a sense of the rhythm of language patterns.

- Do you make time to talk with children when you are not hurried, in a cosy area or maybe when walking outside? Where are children most likely to engage in talk?

- Do you talk with all of the children or just a few?

3. Sharing stories

Enjoying sharing stories, songs, rhymes and games.

(*Birth to Three Matters*)

Babies

Practitioners can share stories, songs, rhymes and games in so many contexts. The range of baby books has been greatly extended from the rag book. There are books that can be used in the bath, clipped to prams and buggies; there are texture and sound books – the range is endless. Use the internet as well as bookshops to collect rhymes and songs. Ask parents what rhymes their babies know and incorporate these into the daily routine as well as sharing the ones used in the setting. Making up games appropriate to the developmental age of the baby is fun. Enjoying these rich resources with an enthusiastic key person can make all the difference to a baby's language development.

Practical activities

- Make a collection of black and white books for the very first few months of growth as black and white is easier for a baby to see.

- Create a book basket – link it to a theme, for example a collection of books that make sounds or have textures, books with animals in.

- Type up the songs you sing with your key person's group. Display the words clearly, create an audio tape or e-mail to parents so that they can share them with the children at home.

- Include songs and instruments from other cultures. Use them regularly, not just at festival times.

- Collect some baby brain music – Bach or Mozart – and play this while watching the babies' responses.

- Singing gently and softly signals sleep or calm-down time. Make sure this is included in the daily routine so that babies begin to recognise and respond to the signal.

- Have a happy song for nappy changing – to distract the babies that do not like the experience.

- Sing outside as well as inside. Do this when you push the buggies and when you stop, sit opposite the baby and sing. Make sure she can see your face, especially your mouth, movements and gestures as she listens to the tone and pitch of your voice.

Toddlers

Toddlers and young children are developing a wide vocabulary and enjoy playing with words and sounds. Learning to listen and memorise are important language skills. Enjoyment, motivation and repetition are key. Many nursery rhymes have survived centuries and this applies to different cultures. It is important to include traditional stories, rhymes and songs from the children's own culture.

Practical activities

- Introduce songs, stories and rhymes from different countries and provide resources or activities to complement them (some multi-language books also come with an audio CD). For example, *Lima's Red Hot Chilli* by David Mills is published in a wide range of languages. Talk with the children and ask why Lima disobeys her mother, who had said 'Don't eat the chilli'. Have they ever been tempted to disobey anyone? Introduce some of the fruits from the story and let them try them.

> **Caution:** Be aware that chillies come in various strengths; some are very hot. Handling them may cause children extreme discomfort.

- Let the children explore the book on their own and tell the story to each other in their own words. Provide a range of 'red hot' colours (reds, oranges, pinks) for the children to paint pictures relating to the story.

- Explore rhyming words through the book *A Squash and a Squeeze* by Julia Donaldson. Help the children to make up their own rhyming words. When saying a familiar nursery rhyme stop before you reach the rhyming word and ask the children to supply the missing word. For example, 'Little Miss Muffet, sat on a . . .' Show the children how to use an audio recorder to say their favourite rhymes and replay them. These cassettes can be taken home to share with their families.

- Construct a simple stage area where the children can dress up and use a microphone/karaoke machine to sing their favourite songs.

- Develop scenarios based on the Gruffalo series by Julia Donaldson or similar favourite stories. The books can be bought with a toy pack and a CD of songs. Encourage the children to create small worlds using the toys, or making their own models, and then to take digital photos that illustrate their creative story-making ideas.

- Use tongue twisters to emphasise a particular initial sound, such as 'Peter Piper picked a peck of pickled peppers'.

- Become familiar with the jingles from children's TV programmes or adverts and encourage the children to share these with each other.

Outcomes for the child

- Babies hear speech and song.
- Babies and toddlers know and can say rhymes.
- Children have fun with language.
- Youngsters learn to listen attentively.

Focus points

As young children reach toddlerhood their language acquisition is developing rapidly; within two more years it will be almost complete. They are able to express their feelings, thoughts and gain information, but language is still closely linked to their social and emotional development. How practitioners respond to their efforts to communicate is crucial. They need to be aware that often young children's speech may not be able to keep up with their thoughts and emotions and this causes them to stumble over words, pause and hesitate or jumble up words. The children need to be given time to respond and know that the adult is patient, attentive and listening to what they have to say.

Staff discussion

- Do all staff have a good knowledge and understanding of language development? Do they need further training in this area?
- Audit resources to identify stories and rhymes that appeal strongly to young children, that will support and stimulate further activities and that include dual languages.

4. Language experience

> ...children begin to use words in their context: e.g. in questioning, imitating with understanding, playing, negotiating.
>
> (*Birth to Three Matters*)

Babies

While babies obviously do not use words in context, they do connect words to situations or to people and in this way show that there must be an understanding beginning in terms of meaning. Babies listen and respond through non-verbal means and they know, for example, that by shaking their head or turning it away they can get across their feelings of either not needing or wanting what is being offered to them. They do imitate their key carers and this engages the adult and reinforces the idea that babies are sociable beings and that listening and responding is occurring without much verbal engagement.

Practical activities

● Spend time looking in a mirror with a baby and see how she responds to 'the baby in the mirror'. It isn't until about 18 months that a baby knows what a sense of self really is. Video or take photographs of this experience.

● At meal or food times babies will often engage more as they have a need. Holding and showing a bottle of milk at feeding time, saying 'Milk' and touching their lips with the teat connects the word with the context and the physical activity. Observe the response. Then on another occasion just show the bottle and observe and finally shake the bottle, say the word and physically touch the baby's lips; from which of these do you get the most response?

- Include questions in the normal pattern of talk such as 'Shall we have a little sleep now?' or 'What is for dinner today?' Create these word patterns and the patterns of rhyme and tone that we use when people ask a question as these are different from when things are just said or reported. This sort of experience initiates a kind of listening and responding game that we all engage in as we communicate with others.

Toddlers

Young children and toddlers are beginning to develop the understanding that the spoken word and text are linked. They are keen to understand the meanings of words and listening to stories helps them to hear words used in context. In their everyday environment they are surrounded by print – in the street, the supermarket and on TV.

Practical activities

- Make a collection of labels that are meaningful to the children such as toy packaging and food cartons. Ask the children if they know where they come from and what was inside the box. Link this to making pictures and signs for resources within the room so that the children can access them, and return them, independently.

- Provide a range of mark-making tools and paper for the children to make their own signs, send messages to each other and write on a large, child-height message board. They can draw, experiment with writing or make symbols. Supply coloured chalks for the children to use outside.

- Set up activities where children can work co-operatively and collaborate with one another. This will increase their language skills. Examples include washing dolls, filling wheelbarrows, pushing and pulling trucks, constructing a car wash.

- During the day take digital photographs of the children engaged in activities. At the end of the day ask the children to tell the group what they were doing. Try to get them to talk about their feelings: did they enjoy it, were there any difficult problems to solve? Encourage the children to use their own words.

- Have a story chair where a child can sit and tell the others a story. Make it look special with a cushion or a drape. The adult can write down the children's stories and make them into a book.

- Choose a special toy, possibly a teddy, and encourage the children to have turns to take it home and on return tell the group what teddy has been doing. Provide a notebook and, if funds allow, a camera for parents to share in and document the experience. The teddy might go on holiday, have a picnic, visit friends or attend a birthday party.

Outcomes for the child

- Speaking and listening develop. Children have a voice.
- Children are able to express themselves more clearly and with confidence.
- Vocabulary increases.

Focus points

Children try out language because they want to communicate; they will make a few mistakes but by interacting with each other and adults they learn to correct them. It is essential that they have real, live communications where others listen to them and respond. The influence of young children learning language by watching TV, such as Teletubbies, is debated world wide. The BBC states that it has fully researched young children's language acquisition in order to develop the programme. At the University of Sheffield, researcher Jackie Marsh (1999) suggests that the formula of using repetition, rhyme and simplicity of language contributes to the programme's success. There has been particular benefit to children with dual language. However, nothing can replace the impact of real-life people talking about real-life things.

Staff discussion

- Do you facilitate and encourage children to talk about real experiences, arrange visits and visitors to increase their experiences?
- Are there areas within the children's environment where you could provide more print, such as big books, posters, signs or symbols? Are there opportunities for text in the outside area – taxi rank, garage markings, car wash, warning signs, information?
- Could the home play area reflect the range of print available in a home – a newspaper (make own), comics, food packaging, mail and parcels, recipes, photo albums, TV programmes?

5. Diverse needs

Children with severe communication difficulties should be encouraged to use non-verbal ways of making contact, and to feel that their attempts to listen and respond are being valued.

(Birth to Three Matters)

Babies

Not all communication difficulties are spotted at birth. Those that are, such as hearing impairment or blindness, present practitioners with the challenge of meeting these children's immediate needs in terms of their care and communication alongside babies whose senses are more developed.

Those caring for a blind baby will need to use their voice more regularly and adopt a more sensitive tone, explaining to the baby in some detail what is happening as they interact with her. A hearing impaired child will benefit from good eye-to-eye contact and facial expressions and gestures from the practitioner. Observations and high quality, consistent practice is crucial. Keeping a good partnership with parents and other agencies is essential.

Practical activities

- Use 'treasure baskets' which contain items with temperature – so that the sense of feelings is focused on. Put in items such as soap stone, real fruit and vegetables, stainless steel measuring spoons. Watch how the baby responds to these and how she tries to communicate any sensations she wants to express to you.

- Use sounds of items, pictures and signs as part of the everyday programme to be inclusive.

- Monitor eye-to-eye contact (children who have a communication problem such as autism may find this difficult; but be cautious – do not make quick judgements about this. Seek expert support after much evidence is gathered). Play eye-to-eye games and engage in eye-to-eye contact often.

- Touching is also a form of contact and so when observing carefully note when a baby uses this as a tool to communicate. When welcoming, comforting or saying 'goodbye' gently touch the face or hands of a baby.

- Practitioners should try to enunciate clearly when speaking to babies, giving them the cleanest, simplest models of speech possible.

- Use lots of repetition. This helps to reinforce the neural pathways that link sound and meaning to a baby's brain. Use rhymes and songs that have repeating lines in them and if possible, use signing or props to aid children as they experience these.

Toddlers

Play is an important tool in the development of the social skills for communication. It provides an enjoyable way for children to interact, listen to each other, seek attention, be accepted and develop their thinking skills. When a key person joins in the play, in a non-threatening way, the learning is taken forward and the practitioner has the opportunity to stop, observe carefully and listen.

Practical activities

- Record children's TV theme tunes, for example 'Bob the Builder', and let the children operate the audio equipment to listen to it whenever they wish. Ask if they recognise the tune, what it means to them and so on. They may be able to tell you about the characters and story.

- Show the children how to use a digital camera and let them capture photos of things that interest them to share with you and other children.

- Use puppets and simple stories to help the children learn the social conventions of greetings, requesting, answering and being polite. Make the stories fun and encourage the children to interact with the puppets. Later let them make their own puppets and stories.

- Devise verbal instructions for the children to carry out. Toddlers aged 1–2 years should be able to respond to a query such as 'Where's teddy?' and a 2- to 3-year-old should be able to follow a two-part instruction such as 'Go to the home corner and bring back teddy'.

- Play the game 'Heads, shoulders, knees and toes', where the children point correctly to the body parts. Some children may not be able to respond quickly so adapt this game to simply pointing to body parts as you name them.

- Play one to one with a child who may be causing concern. Provide a running commentary on what you are doing: 'I am building a tower. You are building a tower'. Pay close attention to how he responds and acknowledge his reply, even if it is hard to understand.

- Repetition and predictability are important features for a child who feels insecure with language. Be prepared to repeat stories, rhymes and replay favourite videos time and again. Encourage the child to talk about them; however, do not ask too many questions – be patient and resist the temptation to finish or complete his sentences.

- Set up collaborative games and co-operative play rather than solitary play to encourage interaction with peers.

Outcomes for the child

- Experiencing language at their pace/with their needs being identified.
- Time to experiment and assimilate language.
- Improved confidence.
- Possibility of initiating an early intervention programme.

Focus points

Although it is crucial that any concerns about a child's communication development are recognised early, it is important not to make snap judgements or assumptions but to observe carefully and gather evidence. Children's language skills vary considerably. The reasons behind language and hearing delays are very complex. Consult with parents and seek professional advice. Be aware that there may be cultural differences surrounding communication that could cause a practitioner to be unduly concerned about a child's language development. For example, in some cultures a sign of respect is to lower your gaze and not make eye contact. Parents may even view a communication delay as a result of 'bad karma' or 'divine punishment'.

Staff discussion

- Invite agencies, for example for the hearing impaired and blind, to talk about how they communicate. Look at what aids they use and how this could assist in everyday good practice.

- Review practitioners' knowledge and understanding of the stages of development for communication and seek training and support from health specialists/speech and language therapists.

- How can you organise space and time for the key person to play on a one-to-one basis with a child showing signs of delayed speech and language development?

- Audit resources and supplement with a wide range of multi-sensory equipment. For example, coloured lights, a light wheel, fairy lights, fibre optics, soft fabrics, saris and a parachute, balloons, aromatherapy smells (lavender), a wide selection of music.

6. Partnership with parents

Involving families and sharing information so that early conversations of babies and older children (either verbal or nonverbal) are celebrated.
(Birth to Three Matters)

Babies

Families are very important to babies and they have different experiences of language as they engage with their family members. Parents will talk to their baby, and so will siblings and their other relations. The level and frequency of talk may differ according to the culture or personalities within the family groupings. Just as families celebrate birthdays it is important that they celebrate language development. Celebrating success when a baby says a word or makes a sound encourages her to communicate.

Practical activities

- Share making a simple language diary with parents. Ask them to share with you photographs or videos of their babies having conversations at home, in their home language.

- Invite grandparents in to talk to their grandchildren and take photos and observations.

- Capture a photograph of the baby making sounds and use this to make a card for Mothering Sunday or Father's Day. If possible, accompany it with an audio tape.

- Ask for home photos of relations talking to a specific child and make them into a book. Laminate and punch a hole in the corner of the picture and call it 'I talked to you today by . . . ' Insert the baby's name.

- Clapping and signalling success such as saying 'Well done' or 'Good girl/boy' reinforces success – make this part of the policy to enhance self-esteem in a baby room.

Toddlers

During the first three years of a child's life he makes huge strides in learning. It is easy to focus on what he hasn't done. However, celebrating his successes with his parents, validating his strengths and interests, will help them to see the uniqueness of their child's development and be proud of his achievements. This can result in an even stronger relationship between the setting and the family.

Practical activities

- Use personal digital assistants (PDAs), tablet PCs or digital cameras to capture children's thoughts and ideas as they engage in daily activities and share these with parents, thus creating a dialogue between family, the practitioner and the children.

- Provide digital cameras so that children can photograph events at home and share these images of their own world with the group using a PC or an interactive whiteboard.

- Ensure that the entrance to the setting is welcoming, gives clear information about the setting and provides a statement on its ethos and philosophy. Display photographs of children engaged in activities annotated with captions that explain the learning taking place.

- Play games with children that require them to listen carefully and respond, for example 'Simon Says', 'London Bridge is falling down' and 'Follow the leader'. These games also help to reinforce position vocabulary through physical activity. Display photographs of these and their basic rules in the welcome/reception area and encourage the parents to play the same games at home.

- Make a collection of the children's favourite songs and rhymes into a booklet that the children can take home with them. Add the children's own illustrations to make them unique and personal.

Outcomes for the child

- Feeling good about communication.
- Instilling a disposition to communicate.
- Being confident to speak to family members and others.
- Knowledge that family and setting are mutually supportive.
- Improved knowledge and understanding of the child leads to better provision.

Focus points

Every family is unique and will celebrate success differently and share the importance and value of making a child gain self-esteem. Think about getting the balance right – celebrating success cannot happen all the time as it loses its meaning. The increase and accessibility of information technology and simple digital cameras means that there are new ways to share communications with parents. This is vital and helps parents understand the learning taking place through everyday activities and play. Many information and communications technology (ICT) devices are portable and allow the children to take them to their activity rather than be tied to a fixed PC. Photographic documentation of a child's learning journey provides tangible evidence for a more focused discussion. It provides an insight into the process of learning rather than the outcome or product; this is especially important in activities such as role play or outdoor physical activity.

Be aware that there may be a number of reasons why parents do not come to the setting, such as timing of sessions, distance and accessibility, language, culture, or even physical barriers within the setting. Some parents may have had negative educational experiences and might be reluctant to come in and talk with practitioners.

Staff discussion

- Review the policy about partnership with parents. Look at how the family plays a part in the communication for babies and toddlers.

- Key persons should plan to talk to parents about how they indicate to babies and toddlers how pleased they are when they develop their speech.

- Equally, if babies and toddlers receive little speech stimulation from their families, this will have an impact on the rate of speech development.

- Use events suggested by agencies like I CAN and Chatter Matters across the setting or even in the home as this can give you an opportunity to share important aspects of communication with parents (see 'Resources').

- Consider how you could use ICT to record and assess children's early language and development of skills and share this with parents.

- Do you operate an informal, open door approach where parents feel comfortable and welcome?

- Are there opportunities for parents to meet their key person for more formal dialogue? Have you explored ways to encourage parental involvement, discovered their skills, experience and interest?

- Ensure that parents give permission for the use of photographs or videos of their child.

References

DfES (Department for Education and Skills) (2002) *Birth to Three Matters: A Framework to Support Children in their Earliest Years*. London: DfES.

DfES (Department for Education and Skills) (2003) *Every Child Matters*. London: DfES.

DfES (Department for Education and Skills) (2005) *Communicating Matters: The Strands of Communication and Language*. London: DfES.

DfES (Department for Education and Skills)/DWP (Department for Work and Pensions) (2003) *National Standards for Under 8s Day Care and Childminding (Full Day Care)*. London: DfES.

Marsh, J. (Aug 1999) 'Education – Teletubbie's teaching tonic', www.news@bbc.co.uk
Rosen, M. (2001) *We're Going on a Bear Hunt*. London: Walker Books.

Resources

Carr, M. (2001) *Assessment in Early Childhood Settings: Learning Stories*. London: Sage Publications.
Donaldson, J. (2003) *A Squash and a Squeeze*. London: Macmillan Children's Books.
Donaldson, J. (2005) *The Gruffalo's Child*. London: Macmillan Audio Books.
Mills, D. (1999) *Lima's Red Hot Chilli*. London: Mantra Publishing.

A discussion forum about dual language children – www.multilinqualchildren.org

Publishers who have a range of dual language books and cultural stories – www.milet.com

'I CAN' project, a charity that helps children to communicate – www.ican.org.uk

I CAN has joined BT to 'Make Chatter Matter' as part of their *Communication Skills for Life* programme. May 2006. See I CAN website.

SHARE, a national family learning programme for pre-schools and nurseries – www.shareuk.org.uk

4 Understanding and being understood

Introduction

Understanding and being understood are not the same and require different skills. Early childhood communication is a two-way process involving a sender and a receiver. The receiver takes in the information and interprets it, then makes sense of it, understands it, according to past experience. Babies, without early language skills, rely on adults to understand and interpret their sounds and gestures. It is essential that parents and practitioners give their attention to babies and young children, showing that they are noticing the child's efforts to communicate by observing and listening carefully. Adults use a sophisticated understanding of codes or signs taking place within a real context in order to make sense of a baby's non-verbal gestures and facial expressions and then deal with them appropriately.

Children need to hear, see and be spoken to clearly in order to make sense of and understand communications. Babies and young children use all their senses to interpret words, gestures, facial expressions and body language. Confusion may be created if the body language does not match the words or tone of voice. Misunderstandings or misinterpretations can cause a child to become upset and frustrated. Depending on the type of communication a child has experienced, the words 'Come here' may mean something good, perhaps bad or possibly interesting. Children brought up with nurturing and loving language develop better learning skills than those who have been subjugated to negative, harsh, short comments such as 'Stop that' or 'Don't do that'.

When young children first enter childcare settings they need to be prepared for the expectations of practitioners and even other children. They will encounter a variety of types of speech when spoken to such as questions that require answers, statements about daily routines, and limits and instructions that have to be followed.

1. Understanding messages

From the very beginning of life, young babies convey messages about what they want and need, as well as how they feel.

(*Birth to Three Matters*)

Babies

Babies communicate to show distress and demand attention, request objects or actions. They show interest in others and respond to others and so understanding and being understood is an important skill they need to develop in their communications with others, whether it is to adults or their peers.

Language can be broken into two areas: receptive language, which is the ability to understand what is said (as in 'making meaning'); and expressive language, which is the ability to put words together into cohesive thoughts in order to express ideas.

Practical activities

● Use the words 'all gone' to show a baby that a bowl is empty or there is no more milk in a bottle – this instant and continual feedback is essential in any learning situation to demonstrate the effects of actions. Posting toys is another resource that could be used to gain an understanding of when something goes away or disappears.

● Have a collection of small boxes with lids and place an unknown and unfamiliar toy in one. Let the baby explore these and observe how she reacts to the new toy, saying its name and hiding it again.

● Provide a picture of an object and then the real object itself. Spend time matching up the pictures and the objects, starting with only two or three items.

- Write babies' names on stickers and attach them to their belongings, for example 'Ann's brush', 'Sam's drink' so youngsters will gain an understanding that items belong to them. They will be more interested in the object and the use of their name gains their attention.

Toddlers

Talk is the introduction to early reading and writing. Toddlers are beginning to be aware of their environment and to understand that signs and labels and the text on products have something to say. They are often keen to make marks themselves, or ask an adult to write for them as they attach meaning to marks. By engaging in first-hand experiences and observations they begin to attach meaning to the words used.

Practical activities

- Take a walk around the local environment. Look for all the signs and labels. Note any signs that give warnings. Encourage the children to talk about what they see. Create simple, clear signs for areas within the setting. Check that the children understand their meaning.

- Discuss all the words used for roads, for example 'paths', 'street', 'avenue'. Do they all mean the same? Encourage the children to learn their own address.

- Help children to think carefully about what they see. Collect pictures of everyday scenes and ask children to tell you what is happening.

- Send and receive messages – give each child their own 'post box'. These can be made simply from strong food cartons, decorated by the children and named. Encourage the children to send each other 'messages'. These can be in any form: mark making, pictures, objects, a flower, a toy.

- Make a collection of holiday postcards – ask why we send them, what do they tell us?

- Find adverts showing two people talking – ask the children to imagine what they are saying to each other. Look for adverts of items the children will know or characters from young children's TV programmes. Put their words into speech bubbles.

Outcomes for the child

- Understanding that they have the ability to convey messages in a non-verbal way which is understood by others.
- Making needs known and understood.
- Knowing they can influence others and they have been understood.
- Beginning to understand that words carry meaning.

Focus points

Think about the strategies a baby uses when she wants something. Research has demonstrated that babies show empathy with others very early in their lives and can show feelings such as jealousy. If babies are misunderstood, consider the impact this could make on their well-being. When young children are starting to communicate, in whatever way they can, it is important for the adult to listen to what they have to say, not how they are saying it, and accept the child's own idiomatic use of language.

Staff discussion

- Ask staff to capture some observations that demonstrate that babies are conveying a message and what happens when it is understood. Now discuss what happens if this was misunderstood; how would they deal with this?
- Discuss with parents what kinds of messages babies convey to them at home.
- Think about the words we use in daily activities and how children may misunderstand them, for example the head's room, gym shoes, cross words.

2. Responding

Respond to what babies show you they're interested in and want to do by providing activities, stories and games.

(Birth to Three Matters)

Babies

Observing babies very carefully, watching their body language and gestures, informs you of their responses to objects and people. They do show what they are interested in by their reactions and when you bring out similar or even the same toy or game they do have an understanding of what will happen next.

Activities, games and stories will need to be as sensory as possible. This assists babies with disabilities and helps to give them an inclusive experience. Having first-hand experiences enables understanding to occur more quickly. Making meaning is a two-way process and there needs to be commitment and excitement on both the baby's and the carer's behalf.

Practical activities

- Babies who like soft toys may enjoy having them in a cosy corner with some small books so they can cuddle the toy and look at a book. Introducing favourites into new experiences acknowledges they have made a choice and that you understand.

- Favourite books may be linked to home experiences. Some children like cats, for example, and they look for 'meow meows' in every book. Make small collections based on babies' interests.

- Try out a range of simple songs and observe very closely which of the ones chosen appears to be enjoyed and understood the most. Make a note of it and share this information.

- 'Peepo' is a well-known game and babies enjoy it. If they show that this is a firm favourite, play this game during routines in recognition that they like it. Make variations of this, for example put a selection or objects onto a tray, cover them with a cloth and use that to play the game.

Toddlers

Toddlers need adults to acknowledge that they have been understood and show a genuine interest in what they are saying by talking with them about the choices they have made. Develop a climate that encourages children's autonomy and initiative yet is supportive. As young children are still self-centred and are struggling for independence this can influence how they approach conflict and problem solving during play. Adults need to help them recognise their own and others' feelings.

Practical activities

- Allow children time to do things for themselves and give them a good range of accessible resources. Recognise and support their interests in TV characters, for example provide small world toys (diggers, dumper trucks, etc.) to connect with Bob the Builder in the sand tray or a floor map for Postman Pat to deliver his parcels.

- Initiate a game of 'Follow my leader' where children take the lead, choosing which actions to perform while the rest follow behind copying what the leader does. Observe which children happily take over the lead role. Are these the same children who appear to be popular, confident and make friends easily?

- Observe children's schema and support their interests, for example for 'transporting' provide a range of bags, purses, wheelbarrows, boxes and objects for them to carry. If it is 'enveloping', have cloths for covering themselves and objects or den making, bags within bags, paper for gluing and paint for covering.

- Provide ways to develop bike play such as car parks with numbered bays, obstacle courses, road safety cones. Have bikes with bells and horns. This shows the children that you are responding to their interests.

Outcomes for the child

- Knowing that they have been understood.
- Building on interests increases well-being and confidence.
- Knowing that messages are valued and received with respect.
- Developing confidence.

Focus points

Think about how the decision on purchasing new games and equipment is made. Is it based on bright catalogue pictures, media marketing, or from seeing what the babies are really interested in first?

Adults may need to rethink how they interact with young children, letting the child take the lead and supporting his interests. Once the adults get to know the children well, the way they think and feel and what interests them, they can support them more effectively. This can result in high levels of involvement and motivation to learn. Look for key messages and signs. Young children's feelings are transparent; they are quick to show when they are bored or uninterested in an activity and when they are totally involved by their non-verbal behaviour. Observe their body language, facial expressions and behaviour to support or modify the activity and help them to succeed and contribute to their sense of well-being.

Staff discussion

- Ask staff to say how they really know when a baby is interested in something. Can they write some clear signals down to share with others?
- Evaluate the current stock of toys available and, based on observation and knowledge of the frequency of use, note which items rarely get used and why.
- Record a session and analyse how you talk to the children. How much do you talk; who do you talk to, how many questions do you ask, how clear are your instructions? How much do you listen and respond to the children?

3. Making opportunities

Provide opportunities for babies to make choices.

(Birth to Three Matters)

Babies

If there are choices available, babies need to make themselves understood as to which they have chosen. This also gives them a range of objects with which to engage and offers new experiences which they may need to make sense of and understand themselves. Restricting choice because 'they are too young and do not understand' is not an enabling viewpoint and has implications for their development.

Health and safety is important in assessing risk when allowing choices, but it requires common sense most of the time. Choices can be easily integrated into routines such as feeding.

Practical activities

- Peas and carrots – babies enjoy eating with their fingers; let them choose between two items first which are very different in colour, texture and size.
- Make a collection of specific items, for example different kinds of balls, spoons or brushes.
- Provide three different teddies or dollies – watch and observe which is the favourite out of the three.
- Have a mobile or play gym with items that have different sounds. Which one do they choose to shake or touch more frequently?

Toddlers

In order for children to make choices they need to be able to make an informed decision and have options. This gives them control over the process. It allows the children to take an active part while the adult takes a step back, intervening only to help the children clarify their thoughts and express their meaning clearly.

Practical activities

- Help children to verbalise ideas by asking 'What would you do if . . . you lost Mummy in a shopping centre? . . . no one came to pick you up? . . . there was no food in your lunch box? . . . the Teletubbies came today? . . . it was snowing – which shoes would you wear?'

- Discuss making difficult choices. Read the story *Would You Rather?* by Jonathan Burningham. For maximum impact, don't show the illustrations for each choice until the children have made up their mind.

- Select software programs such as 'Choose and Tell: Fairy Tales' to help children make decisions (see 'Resources').

- Select two or three books then show them to a small group of children. Draw their attention to the front cover and some of the pages. Ask a child to choose which one you should read. Ask why he chose that one. Ask which character he likes best and why.

- Have one story session where children can choose their favourite story. Vary this by asking them to choose a poem or a song. Support their preferences by providing role-play scenarios, masks and dressing-up clothes that match their favourite stories. Make an audio recording of their favourite stories so they can choose to listen to them whenever they wish.

Outcomes for the child

- Being able to make oneself understood when presented with choices.
- Understanding there are choices.
- Learning how to make decisions and express opinions.

Focus points

An opportunity to choose encourages and promotes confidence and well-being. Presenting choices may mean reorganising the environment, providing duplicate resources and modifying adult involvement.

Staff discussion

- Look at the current opportunities available in the setting for babies and toddlers to make choices. Investigate how babies and toddlers are offered regular daily opportunities for choice.

- Discuss the reality of presenting choices and how current practice could change.

- Look at storage facilities and the range of resources on offer. Purchase trays and containers with subdivisions to allow a selection of objects.

4. Tuning in

Try to 'tune into' the different messages young babies are attempting to convey. Share your interpretations with parents and other staff.

(Birth to Three Matters)

Babies

Attempting to 'tune in to' the different messages that babies are trying to convey needs empathy and close, personal regular contact. For example, understanding and distinguishing between different types of crying becomes clearer as you begin to make connections to times of the day, recognising similar repeated experiences and actions. Feeling that you are unable to tune in to babies' needs can make a practitioner feel inadequate. Sometimes at this time the baby is passed to others in the hope that they can discover why the baby is so distressed. Elinor Goldschmied and Sonia Jackson (1994) advise that the practitioner should focus on slowing down her own breathing. Once the practitioner is calmer and ready to listen intently she should talk quietly and gently to the baby. The baby may not understand what is being said but she will respond to this approach.

Practical activities

- Consider using baby massage techniques in order to use (appropriately) the sense of touch to tune into the baby and promote a feeling of relaxation.

- Avoid using agitated pats, jiggling up and down and using anxious chatter when babies are upset – plan and practise how you will take control of your physical response to a baby's distress or anxiousness. Use other staff to observe and advise you on how well you are doing.

- Using other physical techniques such as 'cradling' to promote 'tuning in', rock babies gently from side to side. Talk softly and try to rock in tandem with the child's moving body. This will promote harmony and closeness.

- Observe facial expressions and other signs as signals that babies make in order to recognise when a baby needs a nappy change and address this need.

Toddlers

As toddlers develop into young children they become more interactive with each other and show an awareness of other children. They recognise and respond to the actions of others, show empathy and kindness when they see another child upset and close friendships are formed. It is also a time when emotions run high and frustrations often lead to tantrums. The children are beginning to know that there are certain rules of behaviour and they can get very upset if another child breaks the rules when playing games.

Practical activities

- Help the children to deal with their conflicting emotions by naming their feelings. Have a small group sit in front of a mirror and pull faces – funny faces, happy, sad, and angry or frightened. Talk about the situations that produce these kinds of faces. Identify the feelings and give them names. Follow up by encouraging them to paint a picture of their choice of a 'feelings face'.

- Recognise that toddlerhood can be a difficult time as they encounter transitions and change. Help them to manage their emotions. Develop an area where children can go and 'chill out' after an emotional outburst. Have comfy cushions, soft toys and some interesting objects for them to investigate.

- Develop a photographic record of children's experiences. Encourage the children to select what they want to record. Later they can recall the experience with other children and with their parents, talking about what they did and how they felt.

- Use digital photographs to record children's individual interests and to plan further support.

Outcomes for the child

- Babies learn that they can have an effect on others.
- Communications are not all verbal.
- Children learn to understand and control their emotions.

Focus points

When children play they are gaining valuable experience about themselves and learning to try out their social skills, relationships and construct meaning from their lives. As they play together they give clear signals to each other that it is all about fun – they laugh and smile, they get excited and use big gestures, sometimes over-acting. By interacting with others they learn that there may be different ways to respond to situations. If they are tired or feeling poorly, it can affect the way they relate to others as they may get irritable or aggressive.

Staff discussion

- Observe and record children's play. Look for examples of how they imitate adults' conversation and actions. Listen to the conversation they have with each other – what do they talk about, how do they express their feelings, what rules do they impose on the play?
- Check your story resources and videos. If necessary, supplement with tales about children's everyday experiences, which reflect their home life and culture, their feelings, worries and concerns.

5. Understanding diverse needs

It is important to be aware that family and culture influence the way in which children's abilities to negotiate and bargain are encouraged.
(Birth to Three Matters)

Babies

Babyhood and the practices of parenting can vary according to family traditions and cultures and it is important to acknowledge and understand this. Being raised from birth as a bilingual poses few problems. Young bilingual learners mix elements of languages with ease. As children associate words with objects, integrating cultural items into play supports them and adds richness to the experience of others who do not share that culture. Appreciate the differences that exist between families and within cultures. Ensure equality of access for both sexes and promote inclusive practices at all times.

Practical activities

- Use 'treasure basket' play but within the contents of the basket include home and cultural artefacts and familiar household items such as cookery items, dishes, spoons.

- Collect samples of materials that reflect cultural patterns and colours. Let the children explore the designs.

- Use a variety of world music as a backdrop for activities, or clap and move to the different rhythms.

- Ensure any visual materials, for example pictures of babies and their parents, reflect the cultural mix in the day care room; if parents are in agreement, use their family photos.

- As babies ask for items, or are anxious, listen to the sounds or words they use. They may be using their mother tongue or 'family word'. Discuss this with parents and clarify which you should use.

Toddlers

Different cultures may have their own traditional ways of raising children, in their expectations of behaviour and their use of discipline. Within families there may be gender preference, hierarchal roles and rules. It is important that children are allowed to respect their family backgrounds and that practitioners focus on and build upon the strengths of each family and not the negatives.

Practical activities

- Create a display showing the children's individual preferences, for example foods, activities, family outings or toys. Talk about the display and help the children to understand that we sometimes like the same things as others but sometimes we like different ones.

- Introduce different items of food at snack time or during cooking sessions. Let the children explore the food, talk about its texture, its smell, shape and colour. Ask them what they think it looks like inside; do they think it will taste sweet or sour? Cut it up and let them try it if they wish to. Encourage the children to talk about the food they eat at home. Collect photographs of different meals and let the children design a paper plate showing their favourite food.

- Ensure that the home play area reflects the diversity of family life and include a range of 'food', cooking utensils, cutlery, clothing, activities. Provide resources that reflect family events – weddings, funerals and celebrations.

- Consult with parents and build up a selection of traditional songs, rhymes and games. Use welcome phrases from children's home language.

- In a small group give each child a stone; tell them it is their pet stone. Make sure that the stones are roughly the same but have distinguishing features. Let the children examine the stones and give theirs a name. After a while collect them up, mix them up and place back on the table. Ask the children to find their stone. A variety of objects can be used in this activity to promote discussion on similarities and differences.

Outcomes for the child

- Valuing own family traditions and culture.
- Learning to explore and appreciate differences.
- Children learn from each other.
- Development of confidence and self-respect.

Focus points

It can be difficult for monolingual or monocultural adults to understand or be aware of the differences between cultures. Some settings may have a very wide variety of languages and religions and a diverse cultural mix. There is not an easy 'one size fits all' approach and you may need to clarify some issues with families or seek external advice. In some cultures it is not usual to have children cared for by non-family adults. Making the transition from home to a childcare setting may cause confusion for some children or they may even feel hostile and insecure. We need to help children to feel secure and proud of their own culture yet ready to accept and learn from others. Practitioners should be aware that children are very adept at picking up messages from adults, not only through what we say but from what we don't say, the tone of our voice, from our non-verbal gestures and our attitudes. We may influence them without intending to. They learn their values from the significant people around them. It is important that adults are free from discrimination and prejudice and that their attitudes and the environment promote positive images of all the children in our society. Even if your local community is an all-white area it is important that children learn that they are part of a wider multi-racial society.

Staff discussion

- Review your Equal Opportunities policy and amend where necessary.
- Children learn their attitudes from everything around them. Audit resources and supplement with appropriate cultural artefacts, toys and items. Check that you have a range of dual language books, and that the stories challenge stereotypes and build positive images. Supply paint and paper in a full range of skin colours.
- Discuss how you can provide opportunities for children to talk positively about the similarities they have with their friends and acknowledge the differences.
- Observe the way non-English children try to gain attention. Recognise, appreciate and respond.
- Organise home visits before and during the first weeks of childcare to help ease the transition and to build a partnership with parents.

6. Communicating meaning

For a child with a language impairment or communication disorder, sharing meaning is important; e.g. using a combination of signs and words.

(Birth to Three Matters)

Babies

Each baby is unique and their individual development will vary so using stage based developmental guidelines can only form part of the whole picture. Albert Einstein did not begin to talk until he was three! Documentation and supporting evidence in the form of high quality observations can help the practitioner when talking to parents about any causes for concern. Some settings use baby sign language as an 'add on' to existing practice in order to give babies another way of communicating. This practice, though, needs to be used consistently across the setting. The parents of the children involved also need to be fully informed of this practice.

Practical activities

- As part of the general practice include activities which involve eye-to-eye contact (a lack of eye-to-eye contact is linked to autism).

- Hold the baby on your lap or in a baby chair/rocker and say her name. Play 'Peepo' and monitor her eye movements.

- Make a picture book relating to a baby's needs – share it with her, showing, saying and pointing to the pictures using images such as a feeding bottle, food, teddy, etc.

- Bouncing balloons – seat the baby carefully and using a balloon, watch the baby's eyes widen as she follows the balloon bobbing up and down.

- Rippling ribbon – use a wooden spoon with lots of colourful ribbons on it. Have a second one with small bells (such as those that go on a cat's collar); move and shake the spoon to make sounds. Observe the baby's responses. Does she appear to react to the sight and sounds of the spoons?

- With visually impaired babies use your voice to describe what you are doing. Build up resources linked with sounds such as a 'sound treasure basket', toys that move or pop up and make sounds.

Toddlers

If a toddler is having difficulties communicating, it may be due to a delay in hearing, speech or visual development. Practitioners have many opportunities to check whether children are having difficulties. Early identification, discussions with parents and seeking external professional advice, assessment and support are key to meeting children's individual needs. If a child is experiencing difficulties, it is essential that adults are calm and patient as he can get very upset and frustrated while trying to communicate.

Practical activities

- Engage all the senses and observe the children's responses. Develop a 'smelly box' with herbs, spices and different aromas. Make a wall panel of different textures for the children to feel. Provide **Caution:** Some strong spices may cause irritation a variety of tactile activities such as rolling out dough, modelling with clay, mark making in corn flour, catching bubbles. Some research suggests that visually impaired children can see orange, lemon and lime colours better than others.

- Take advantage of weather to provide experiences that connect with senses: the sound of the wind, the feel of rain on their cheek, splashing in puddles, making mud pies or playing with snow.

- Visually impaired children need extra stimuli to help them engage in an activity, for example throwing a bean bag to hit a tambourine so that they know when they have 'scored'. Help them to recognise and discriminate sounds around them by listening carefully and naming them – a dripping tap, a clock ticking or trying to identify different adults by their footsteps. Listen to quiet sounds, ones that keep on going or keep coming back. Find peaceful sounds, annoying sounds and warning sounds. Find words to describe them such as 'sharp', 'dull', 'soft' or 'hard'.

- Adults may find it useful to use exaggerated body language and gestures when communicating with a non-verbal child. Try to use pictures, symbols and real objects to reinforce your speech or make sure the object is within view, for example 'fetch your coat'. Play musical games that involve touch such as 'Hands, knees and bumps-a-daisy'.

- Introduce the non-verbal child to remote-controlled toys so that he can experience the feeling of taking control.

Outcomes for the child

- Developing confidence.
- Feeling of belonging and connecting with peers.
- Learning to communicate in different ways.

Focus points

Around 250,000 children under five have speech and language problems. These may be difficulties in talking, expressing themselves or understanding, or both. There are systems such as Makaton that use signs and symbols to help children who are having difficulty.

Staff discussion

- Are all adults aware of the Code of Practice for special educational needs (DfE, 1994)?

- If adults are concerned about a child's progress in communication, arrange a day when all adults focus on observing the child during one session and then compare notes. They can record how the child responds to activities, different adults, various times of the day, indoors/outdoors, solitary play and collaborative play.

- Identify if practitioners require further training to help with the diverse needs of children in their care.

- Discuss how adults provide opportunities for children to develop concepts and talk about children who are different from themselves.

References

Burningham, J. (1994) *Would You Rather?* London: Red Fox Picture Books.

DfE (Department for Education) (1994) *Code of Practice on the Identification and Assessment of Special Educational Needs.* London: Central Office of Information.

DfES (Department for Education and Skills) (2002) *Birth to Three Matters: A Framework to Support Children in their Earliest Years.* London: DfES.

DfES (Department for Education and Skills) (2003) *Every Child Matters.* London: DfES.

DfES (Department for Education and Skills) (2005) *Communicating Matters: The Strands of Communication and Language.* London: DfES.

DfES (Department for Education and Skills)/DWP (Department for Work and Pensions) (2003) *National Standards for Under 8s Day Care and Childminding (Full Day Care).* London: DfES.

Goldschmeid, E. and Jackson, S. (1994) *People Under Three: Young Children in Daycare.* London: Routledge.

Choose and tell fairytales – www.chooseandtellseries.com

Resources

Makaton Vocabulary Development Project – www.makaton.org/

Conclusion

Although babies are born with a desire to communicate, unless they receive sensitive responses to their initial attempts at language this development may be delayed. The activities in this book have been designed to help children grow into sociable human beings by promoting effective two-way interactions between their peers and adults. Many of the activities encourage a fun approach, are rooted in play, yet stimulate the developing mind. When actively engaged children will use all their senses to interpret and respond appropriately to communication signals. In these early years their communication skills will go from babbling to fluency, from purely oral language to print and mark making.

Children have an innate need to communicate their thoughts, ideas and feelings and through the skilful support of an adult they can become empowered, learn to express themselves freely and be accepted into positive relationships. They develop into their own unique personalities. For many reasons some young children do not receive the opportunities and language development at home that professionals in the field of early years would like to see, therefore your role in supporting children's communication is particularly important and may well make a difference to a child's long-term development.

Appendix: The Birth to Three Framework for 'A Skilful Communicator'

A Skilful Communicator

Being Together

Being a sociable and effective communicator

Including
- Gaining attention and making contact
- Positive relationships
- Being with others
- Encouraging conversation

Finding a Voice

Being a confident and competent language user

Including
- The impulse to communicate
- Exploring, experimenting, labelling and expressing
- Describing, questioning, representing and predicting
- Sharing thoughts, feelings and ideas

Listening and Responding

Listening and responding appropriately to the language of others

Including
- Listening and paying attention to what others say
- Making playful and serious responses
- Enjoying and sharing stories, songs, rhymes and games
- Learning about words and meanings

Making Meaning

Understanding and being understood

Including
- Communicating meaning
- Influencing others
- Negotiating and making choices
- Understanding each other

© DfES (2002) *Birth to Three Matters: A Framework to Support Children in their Earliest Years*

David Fulton Publishers

helping children to be strong

Ann Roberts and Avril Harpley

This essential book covers the key areas of:

- Me, myself and I
- Being acknowledged and affirmed
- Developing self-assurance
- A sense of belonging

Ann Roberts is an independent consultant and author. Avril Harpley is an experienced nursery inspector. She works as a consultant with schools in their early years departments.

£10.00 • Paperback • 80 pp • 1-84312-451-3 •May 2007

Other titles in the series!

Linked directly to the government's **"Birth to Three Matters Framework"** (DfES 2002), this handy little series of books provide direct advice, information and ideas on how to implement the framework into your early years setting.

Easy to read and digest at your own pace, then to implement or share with your team, the **"From Birth to 3" Series** will prove invaluable to all those with responsibility for the care and education of children in the early years settings.

NEW "From Birth to 3 series"

Each book includes:

- Practical activities to support the area of learning
- Outcomes for the child
- Professional focus points
- Ideas for staff discussion

The "From Birth to Three" series will prove invaluable to all those with the responsibility for the care and education of children in early years settings.

Ordering your books couldn't be easier!
For more details visit www.fultonpublishers.uk